THE MATTER OF ZEN

The Zen meditation of the Mahayana
Is beyond all our praise.
Giving and morality and the other perfections,
Taking of the name, repentence, discipline,
And the many other right actions,
All come back to the practice of meditation.

HAKUIN, *"Song of Zazen"*

The matter of

ZEN

A brief account of **ZAZEN** by Paul Wienpahl

New York University Press   1964

For Zuigan Goto Roshi

CONTENTS

PREFACE

THIS BOOK concerns the *practice* of Zen Buddhism. The practice is a particular form of meditation. In Japan, the only country in which it is any longer seriously pursued, the practice is called *zazen*.

I am endeavoring to direct attention to *zazen* because it is being overlooked in the current interest in Zen. My purpose is not to provide a manual of *zazen*. Adequate instruction in this practice requires a teacher. The present volume may be regarded as though the author were a man who is pointing and shouting, "Hey, look!" when his fellows do not see the tiger lurking in the bushes.

I have had a secondary reason for writing, which will be no more than mentioned. It is that of taking some of the mystery out of mysticism. For mysticism appears to me simply as a radical form of empiricism or common sense to which we can all pay attention with profit. Mysticism is not something incomprehensible or supernatural. It is only rare—though its scarcity has helped to make it seem mysterious.

Throughout the book when the word 'zen' is capitalized, it is being used as an abbreviation for the phrases 'Zen Buddhist' or 'Zen Buddhism.' When it is not capitalized, it is used to designate a kind of study at the basis of which is the practice of *zazen*. A mystique has grown up in the use of the word 'zen' that has caused it to be used alone with practically no sense. This has helped to obfuscate what is otherwise simple. It has also lent mystery where there is naught but hard work and unflagging effort.

A word about the style in which this book is written. Zen Buddhist masters have since ancient times used a peculiar common-folk dialect. Translations of Zen texts and books about Zen do not usually reflect this vernacular and the frequent coarseness of the speech. They thus miss some of the earthiness that characterizes Zen Buddhism. Wherever it has been natural, therefore, I have used abbreviations, slang, and a deliberate curtness of expression. Not in imitation, but to convey the character of Zen Buddhists, which has been reflected in their own manner of speech.

I wish to thank the publishers of the works referred to in the text for permission to quote from their books. Thanks are also due to Mr. and Mrs. Herbert Fingarette and to my wife for reading the manuscript and for offering a number of helpful suggestions.

Without the kindness and instruction of Mrs. Ruth Sasaki, Mr. Walter Novick, and other members of The First Zen Institute of America in Kyoto this book would not have been possible. I wish further to thank Mrs. Sasaki and Mr. Novick for making possible something far more important than a book. Mrs. Sasaki also read the manuscript and made a number of helpful comments.

Santa Barbara

June, 1963

THE MATTER OF ZEN

1

The first step

AMONG Zen Buddhists there is an old saying that Zen cannot be transmitted in books. On the other hand, Zen literature is voluminous and a great deal has been written about Zen. The question naturally arises: What accounts for this paradox?

The answer is simple, although, like all things that are perfectly obvious, it is at the outset obscure. The reason why Zen cannot be transmitted in books or by words in any form is implied by the very name of this form of Buddhism. For 'zen' means meditation. Zen Buddhism is literally Meditation Buddhism. And meditation cannot be transmitted in books any more than swimming or any other physical practice can. On the other hand, both meditation and the experience in which it results can be described in words, just as swimming can; in neither case, however, should the description be confused with that of which it is the description. This is obvious in the matter of swimming. It has been far less obvious with Zen Buddhism.

From the foregoing, it follows that a person can learn more about Zen in a half hour of meditating than he can by reading a dozen books. It also follows, however, that, if a person is practicing meditation, words in the form of lectures, stories, or even books might help him with his understanding of Zen by helping him to improve his meditation practice. Because this is so, the literature of Zen is large and Zen teachers are by no means mute.

Later it will become clear that the practice of Zen Buddhism is characterized by steps. Meditation may be likened to an onion. It has layers and, like those of the onion, they resemble each other and yet are distinct. One can penetrate ever more deeply into meditation although the same thing is always going on. The zen student, a person engaged in zen practice, finds that he makes steps forward in improving his meditation—or, as one might say, in his understanding of Zen Buddhism. The thing does not come all at once any more than walking does.

For the Westerner who is serious about studying Zen, the first of these steps must consist in seeing the obvious fact that Zen Buddhism is *Meditation* Buddhism. He must see that the heart of the matter is a practice. No amount of reading that he can at present do will prepare him for this step, unless the reading is deliberately designed for this purpose as is the present volume. Even then it is likely that without some actual practice the step will be faltering. To what extent does a person know sailing who has never sailed?

Zen Buddhism, then, is Meditation Buddhism. The word 'zen,' as one often reads, comes from the Chinese *'ch'an,'* which comes from the Sanscrit *'dhyana,'* which means meditation. That which characterizes Zen sects and differentiates them from other Buddhist sects is the strict reliance of their adherents on the practice of meditation as the method for achieving the goal of all Buddhists: enlightenment or freedom.[1]

'Zen' means meditation. *This cannot be repeated too often.* 'Meditation' in this context means sitting quietly, more specifically, sitting in a certain way and breathing in a certain manner. It may mean more, for meditation has layers; but basically 'zen' means meditation and that is sitting quietly and breathing quietly. A person studies Zen Buddhism by meditating (sitting). He may perform other activities, like receiving instruction from a *roshi* or Zen teacher and practicing a certain moral code.[2] However, these other things are all adjuncts to meditation. They are devices for improving it. They are in a sense parts of meditation. Nevertheless, the practice is meditation and the *goal* is meditation.

As the great Japanese Zen teacher of the thirteenth century, Dogen, had it: practice *is* enlightenment.[3] The zen student takes a step when he sees this too. Then he is more contented with meditation even though he may not have penetrated deeply into it.

In Japanese Zen Buddhist circles it is said that 'zen' is an abbreviation of '*zazen*.' Because the word 'meditation' and its variants are misleading in this connection by reason of their Western and Christian associations, I shall hereafter refer only to *zazen*. In order to make clear that to which this term basically refers, the next chapter is a description of *zazen*. It is taken from Dogen's, which is the classic description, although the portion in it about counting breaths comes from my own instructor. It is one of the aids for *zazen,* of which more later.

"The monk Fu, of T'ai-yuan, was first a Buddhist scholar. When he was lecturing on the Parinirvana Sutra while in Yang-chao, a Zen monk happened to stay in his temple and attend the lecture. Fu began discoursing on the Dharmakaya, which incidentally invoked the Zen monk's laugh. Afterwards Fu invited the monk to tea and asked: 'My scholarship does not go very far, but I know I have faithfully expounded the

4

meaning in accordance with the literary sense. Having seen you laugh at my lecture, I realize that there must have been something wrong. Be pleased to give me your kind instruction in this.'

"The Zen monk said: 'I simply could not help laughing at the time, because your discourse on the Dharmakaya was not at all to the point.'

"Fu asked: 'Where am I wrong?'

"The monk told him to repeat his lecture, whereupon Fu began thus: 'The Dharmakaya is like vacuity of space, it reaches the limits of time, it extends to the ten quarters, it fills up the eight points of the compass, it embraces the two extremes, heaven and earth. It functions according to conditions, responds to all stimulations and there is no place where it is not in evidence . . .'

"The monk said: 'I would not say that your exposition is all wrong, but it is no more than a talk about the Dharmakaya. As to the thing itself, you have no knowledge.'

"Fu: 'If this be the case, tell me what it is?'

"Monk: 'Would you believe me?'

"Fu: 'Why not?'

"Monk: 'If you really do, quit your lecturing for a while, retire into your room for about ten days, and, sitting up straight and quietly, collect all your thoughts, abandon your discriminations as regards good and bad, and see into your inner world.'" [4]

5

2

Zazen

SELECT for your *zazen* a quiet, dimly lit room. Garb yourself in loose clothing and obtain several large cushions. Arrange these on a bench or on the floor so that you can sit comfortably on them. Seat yourself cross-legged on the cushions. If you can so cross your legs that the right foot rests on the left thigh and the left foot on the right thigh, so much the better. This is called the lotus position. It is, however, a difficult position to assume, and you may satisfy yourself at first with getting only one foot on one thigh (i.e., half into the position), or by simply sitting American Indian fashion.

Use a cushion to raise your rump above the level of your legs. It is important to get a stable and comfortable seat. Keep your back straight and erect; your hands in your lap, the left hand, palm upward, on the right palm, with the tips of the thumbs joining. Your head too is erect, the ears in the plane of the shoulders and the nose in that of the navel. Keep your eyes open and fix them unfocused on a point on the floor. This point is about two feet in front of you if you are seated on the floor. Raise the whole body slowly and quietly, move it repeatedly to the left and to the right, forward and around, until the proper seat and a straight relaxed posture are assured.

Now that you are seated, commence to breathe in the following manner. Breathe through the nose. Inhale as much as you require, letting the air come in by distending the diaphragm. Do not draw it in, rather let it come to you. Then exhale slowly. Exhale completely, getting all of the air out of your lungs. As you exhale slowly count 'one.' Now inhale again. Then exhale slowly to the count of 'two.' As so on up to 'ten.' Then repeat . . .

You will find this counting difficult as your mind will wander from it. However, keep at it, striving to bring your mind back to the process of counting. As you become able to do this with reasonable success, start playing the following game with the counting. As you count 'one' and are slowly exhaling, pretend that that 'one' is going down, down, down into your stomach. Then think of its being down there as you inhale and begin to count 'two.' Bring the 'two' down and place it (in your imagination, one might say) in your stomach beside the 'one.' . . . Eventually you will find that your mind itself, so to speak, will descend into your stomach.

Gradually it will become possible for you to concentrate with more and more success on the numbers. Your mind will wander. You will find yourself carried away on trains of thought, but you will have increasing success in bringing your mind back to the counting. Do not try to keep the "alien" thoughts out. Try, instead, to concentrate on the counting. If necessary, take note of the thoughts as they come in and then return to the counting. Get rid of the thoughts, as it were, not by pushing them out of your mind, but by concentrating on the counting. Eventually you will be able to be quiet in both body and mind, and you will have learned how busy your mind ordinarily is. In later *zazen,* after instruction from a *roshi* has commenced, the zen student concentrates on a koan (a special kind of problem) instead of counting. Finally there is just the sitting.

Zen students often commence practicing *zazen* in two-hour periods, breaking off every half hour to walk briskly around. After some practice the length of these periods is extended and the adept student goes without breaks. However, even the more experienced zen student will not hesitate to interrupt his *zazen* with a quick walk when he finds himself growing drowsy or too stiff.

As mentioned previously, *zazen* may be likened to an onion. It has many layers, and they are in a sense all the same. If you were to bore through an onion, from one side to the other, the first layer would be like the last and both like the center. So is the first sitting like the last—and yet, of course, they are different.

To bore through an onion you require a tool. Almost any tool will do, but some work better than others for this particular purpose. And so in the practice of *zazen* there are tools that may be called aids to *zazen*. There is counting. There are koans. There are lectures from the *roshi*. There are exercises for limbering the muscles. There is the practice of a moral code. And so on.

These aids to *zazen* should not be confused with *zazen*. The "philosophy" of Zen Buddhism should never be confused with Zen Buddhism. And yet *zazen* and the aids to *zazen* become inextricably linked. The foregoing remarks about *zazen* show this. Actually this chapter should have been shorter. It should have read: *Zazen* is sitting quietly.

Nevertheless, the aids and the practice coalesce. The practice of a moral code to deepen *zazen* becomes simply the practice of a moral code for its own sake. The enlightened man, the man who practices *zazen,* finally behaves morally because he is moral and not because he is told to do so or because he thinks that he ought to or even because he wants to. He has started into the onion and gone through it and come to the other surface. He behaves just as he did before, but now there is a difference—in him.

[1]   IN the *Avatamsaka Sutra* a teacher, Sucandra, replies to a student as follows:

"Sucandra: That is not so. Self-realization never comes from mere listening and thinking. O son of a good family, I will illustrate the matter by analogy. Listen! In a great desert there are no springs or wells; in the springtime or in the summer when it is warm, a traveller comes from the west going eastward; he meets a man and asks him: I am terribly thirsty; pray tell me where I can find a spring and a cool refreshing shade where I may drink, bathe, rest, and get thoroughly revived?

"The man from the east gives the traveller, as desired, all the information in detail, saying: When you go further east the road divides itself into two, right and left. You take the right one, and going steadily further on you will surely come to a fine spring and a refreshing shade. Now, son of a good family, do you think that the thirsty traveller from the west, listening to the talk about the spring and the shady trees, and thinking of going to that place as quickly as possible, can be relieved of thirst and heat and get refreshed?

"Sudhana: No, he cannot; because he is relieved of thirst and heat and gets refreshed only when, as directed by the other, he actually reaches the fountain and drinks of it and bathes in it."

[2]   "A STUDENT of Tendai, a philosophical school of Buddhism, came to the Zen abode of Gasan as a pupil. When he was departing a few years later, Gasan warned him: 'Studying the truth speculatively is useful as a way of collecting preaching material. But remember that unless you meditate constantly your light of truth may go out.'"

[3]   IN a way, practicing Zen is like living. No one can live for another, though he may give pointers that help.[1]

3

Aids to zazen

IN his *Essays on Zen Buddhism,* Mr. Suzuki says
that *satori* is the alpha and omega of Zen. This may be true
when properly understood. However, even then it can be misleading, particularly for Westerners. For the heart of Zen
Buddhism is zen, which is *zazen.* Language does not deceive
us here. And when Mr. Suzuki goes on to define *satori* as an
intuitive looking into the nature of things in contradistinc-
tion to the analytical or logical understanding of it, he is
probably still right. However, the phrase 'intuitive looking,'
inevitably suggests something mysterious and esoteric. In this
sort of talk we easily miss the simple fact of *zazen.* A person

comes to look intuitively into things when he does *zazen*. Only this seems and is so commonplace that we of the West cannot believe that this is it.

I have said that there are various aids to *zazen,* for example, the koan exercise and the practice of a moral code.[1] There are many others. Let's consider a few that may serve to take some of the mystery out of something that is actually simple and practical although it is rare because it requires hard work and unremitting effort.

The description of *zazen* in Chapter 2 might be said to describe formal *zazen*. In a Zen temple compound, formal *zazen* is practiced in a building set aside for this purpose, called the *zendo*. Here the zen student sits for hours every day, pursuing his "studies." However, it soon becomes apparent that there is another kind of "sitting," which might be called informal *zazen,* and awareness of this fact helps the student with his *zazen*.

Informal *zazen* can be performed in any position and during many simple activities. It consists mainly in carrying over into these activities the attitudes of quiet, concentration, and aware- ness *and* the quiet, concentration, and awareness that come to mark formal *zazen*.[2] Thus, *zazen* can be performed, for example, while seated in a chair, while picking weeds, or while sweep- ing the floor. Because there is informal *zazen* a person can have his zen study pervade much of his waking life and, indeed, in a sense his sleep. At first it is useful to try this. Then it becomes no longer a matter of trying; it is simply done. A Zen Buddhist once said: when I eat, I eat; when I sleep, I sleep.

There are, then, one might say, degrees of *zazen*. This fact has some bearing on the position used in formal *zazen*. *Zazen* gets more formal, so to speak, as the lotus position is approximated. In this position the arms and legs are "turned in" and point to the stomach, which becomes the center of the student's being. This has the effect of intensifying his concentration and in a way coordinates his entire body with his breathing. The position has, furthermore, the merit of great stability when properly assumed. The two knees and the buttocks form the base of a triangle. In this position one becomes like the triangle depicted here. One has a firm base. The center of gravity is low. There is stability and repose as well as concentration in the position. The figure is not top- or mind-heavy.

The position in fact symbolizes and in a way is the goal of *zazen*. A person can, of course, practice *zazen* sitting in a chair with his feet dangling to the floor. However, when you compare the figure suggested by this position with that of the triangle planted firmly on the floor or on a rock in the garden, you get a feeling for the greater concentration, repose, stability, and quiet of the latter. You see that the chair-sitter will not penetrate very deeply with his meditation.

Now in fact the isosceles triangle with its perpendiculars dropped not only portrays the goal of *zazen;* it can be used by the zen student as something on which he can concentrate from time to time to improve his *zazen.*[3] He tries to become like that triangle: firmly based and solid. He is trying to get his own "center of gravity" down into his middle, into his guts, or in the language used above, into the center of his being. Imagining the triangle helps him to do this.

In a way zen study or *zazen* is as simple as the foregoing. One is striving in it to become like that triangle. This is, of course, not the all of it. However, the more of it is just as simple and no less without mystery. Consider, for example, another figure that also portrays the goal of *zazen* and is at the same time, when emulated, *zazen* itself.

The Japanese have a toy called *Daruma*. The name is the Japanese version of 'Bodhidharma,' the name of the founder of Zen Buddhism in China. A *Daruma* is a small round doll with a weighted base. It is in effect a figure of Bodhidharma seated in meditation, and it has within it a bell that sounds whenever the doll is moving about and not settled in the upright position. Because of the weight in its base, the doll "seeks" to arrive at and maintain the upright position whenever it is disturbed. Otherwise it sits calmly without making a sound. The

16

principle according to which it works is familiar to us as it is used in Western toys.

How does this toy "describe" *zazen* or Zen Buddhism? When *Daruma* is undisturbed he sits quietly and has nothing to "say." When he is disturbed, when, so to speak, something in his environment influences him, he "responds." He can roll with the punches. His response is such as to return him always to

the upright, calm position. Part of his response is the tinkling of his bell. It is as though he were grumbling about the disturbance. Or it is as though he were talking or thinking his way out of his difficulty. When the difficulty disappears, when he has succeeded in regaining his equilibrium, when he is at one with his world, he ceases from complaining or from talking and thinking. These, one sees from the doll, are just ways of resuming one's balance, and when they are no longer necessary one no longer uses them.

Sitting quietly, *Daruma* represents the condition of no-mind of which there is so much said in connection with Zen Buddhism and yet which is as simple as the doll *shows*. In a way it is just being quiet. It is also being able to sway in the "storms" and return to an even keel. It is also being able to use the practical means that we have for doing this, such as thought.

In his little book *How We Think* and elsewhere, the instrumentalist John Dewey proposed the view that thinking and the speech that accompanies it are problem-solving devices. Thinking occurs when a problem confronts us. It ceases when the problem is solved and, in Dewey's language, on-going activity is resumed. One might say that the philosopher is he who thinks too much, who thinks when there are no real problems. He thus becomes top-heavy. There are other ways of regarding the philosopher and they have their uses. But this one helps with seeing what *zazen* is. It is a practice that helps to keep one from thinking when it is unnecessary. It is a device for being practical, that is, for keeping the head out of the clouds —a condition in which a person is highly unstable. The *Daruma* doll symbolizes this and is worth keeping in mind from time to time as an aid to achieving that quietness which is both the goal and the practice of *zazen*.

It should be added, and a person senses this when he tries *zazen,* that the quiet of *zazen* is not the quiet of retreat and lassitude. It takes much hard work and great effort of will to do *zazen*. That work and that effort are as much a part of *zazen* as is the quiet. Think only again of *Daruma.* He does not spring immediately to the upright position when disturbed. He rocks about and in fact requires great force to reach and maintain his balanced position. There is that weight in his bottom that exerts the force, just as there must be the force in a man that keeps him on an even keel.

The remainder of this book concerns aids to *zazen*. When abstractions creep in and philosophy lays on, they are pointers to *zazen*.

4

Further directions

KEIZAN, a Japanese who lived not long after Dogen, made the latter's basic directions for *zazen* (Chapter 2) more explicit by setting forth certain rules to observe while practicing *zazen*. When it is noticed that these rules (some of which are given in the present chapter) can be applied to informal as well as to formal *zazen*, something vital about *zazen* is seen: its rules are rules for living. A few others of Keizan's rules are also reproduced here for amusement's sake. A person can get too serious about *zazen*.[1]

Think neither of good nor evil.

Those who would clear up their minds (i.e., get them quiet)

must abandon complex thinking and forsake the world and Buddhism.

Free yourself from trifles like techniques and fortune-telling. Avoid singing, dancing, music, noisy chatter, gossip, publicity, and profit-seeking. Although composing verses and poetry may help to quiet your mind, do not become too involved with them.

Avoid beautiful robes. A beautiful robe gives rise to desire, and there is in it, too, danger of theft. If someone happens to offer you a rich robe, turn it down. If you have such a robe, discount its importance.

Wear old clothes, but mend them and keep them clean. If they are not clean, your chances of getting sick increase and this obstructs training.

In eating, avoid anything unripe, indigestible, rotten, or unsanitary. Such food will make your stomach rumble and disturb your *zazen*. And do not fill up with delicacies. Such gorging will not only increase your discomfort during *zazen*, but will show everyone that you are not yet free from avarice. Food exists only to support life; do not cling to the taste of it.

Avoid *zazen* right after breakfast or lunch.

In preparing for *zazen*, take cold-preventing medicine, sesame seed, and mountain potatoes. In actually doing *zazen*, do not lean against walls, backs of chairs, or screens. Stay away from high places with strong winds even if the view is good. This is a fine way to get sick.

Any excesses lead to a disturbed mind. Anything that puts a strain on body and mind becomes a source of illness. Thus, do not practice *zazen* where there is danger of flood, fire, strong winds, and robbery. Keep away from areas near the seashore, bars, red-light districts, homes of widows and young virgins, and theaters. Avoid living near ministers, kings, and high authority or gossips and seekers after fame and profit.

Temple rituals and buildings have their worth. But if you are concentrating on *zazen* avoid them. Do not get attached to sermons and instructions because they disturb your mind. Do not take pleasure in attracting crowds or gathering disciples. Shun a variety of practices and studies. Do not do *zazen* where it is too light or too dark, too hot or too cold.

5

Simplicity I

THERE is talk of the life of the spirit. In the literature on Zen Buddhism we read of the transmission of Mind. When this spiritual thing is not just the life of letters, the life of the intellect, what is it?

One day I told the *roshi* how my legs ached during *zazen*. He joked about this. He said that my mind was as stiff as my legs and the rest of my body, that a supple body goes with a supple mind. He continued:

You should keep up your "work" when you return to the United States. That is, sit, do *zazen* for twenty minutes or a half hour a day. That is enough if it be done regularly. It will relax you and you will sleep better. That gives *you* twenty-three and a half hours a day, and a half hour for your spiritual life. After a while that half-hour will spread. Not that you will sit any more, but its effect will come to pervade your ordinary life.

Thus can the mystery go out of the word 'spirit.'
Sitting quietly and finally living quietly are the spiritual life. Just deepen the quiet. The high-sounding words are only pointers to it. Of course, one does not get far with so little effort as a half hour a day. On the other hand, the fact that a man will never run a four-minute mile is no reason why he should not learn to walk.

6

Simplicity II

"BOKUJU (Mu-chou), who lived in the latter half of the 9th Century, was once asked, 'We have to dress and eat every day, and how can we escape from all that?' The master replied, 'We dress, we eat.' 'I do not understand you,' said the questioner. 'If you do not understand, put your dress on and eat your food.' " [1]

Zazen is also hard because a person keeps looking for extraordinary results, whereas the results are natural. It is difficult to accept this.

"Ryutan Shin stayed with Tenno Go (748–807) for three years, but having no instruction in Zen as he expected, he asked, 'It is some time since my arrival here, but I have yet had no words from you, O master, in the way of spiritual teaching.' Said the master, 'Ever since your arrival here I have been teaching you in matters of spiritual enlightenment.' Ryutan did not understand this and asked again, 'When were such matters ever imparted to me?' The master's reply was, 'When you bring me tea to drink, do I not take it? When you bring me my food to eat, do I not accept it? When you bow to me, do I not acknowledge it by nodding? When was I ever at fault in instructing you in matters spiritual?' Dogo stood for a while thinking about it. The master said, 'If you want to see into the matter, see it at once; deliberation makes you miss the point forever.' This is said to have awakened the disciple to the truth of Zen." [2]

"When a monk came to Dogo Chi (779–835) and asked, 'What is the deepest secret you have finally come to?' Dogo came down from his chair, bowed to the visitor and said, 'You are welcome, indeed, coming from afar, but I am sorry I have not much to entertain you with.' " [3]

"Gensha mounted the seat and after a moment of silence gave this out: 'Do you know it? Do you now recognize it?' So saying, he went back to his room. Another time after a silence he simply said, 'This is your true man, just this.' Still another time his silence was followed by this, 'Daruma is present right here, right now. Do you see him, O monks?'

"On another occasion he was a little better, for he gave this

after a period of silence: 'I am doing what I can for your edification, but do you understand?' " [4]

"As Nansen (Nan-ch'uan) declared, it (Zen) is your 'everyday
thought.' When later a monk asked a master what was meant
by 'everyday thought,' he said,

" *'Drinking tea, eating rice,*
  I pass my time as it comes;
  Looking down at the stream, looking up at the mountains,
  How serene and relaxed I feel indeed!' " [5]

The matter-of-factness of the matter cannot be overempha-
sized. A person keeps thinking that it is something else, something more. It is just a man shopping with his wife without irritation. The only thing that makes it more is the enormous amount of effort that is required to achieve this simple
state.

7

Sanzen and the koan

A CHARACTERISTIC of *zazen* is its simplicity. A characteristic of the spiritual life is its simplicity. Both are uncomplicated and neither are beyond the reach of anyone. These statements are true. However, they can be misleading, for *zazen* is also enormously hard work.

Being quiet for prolonged periods requires great effort. Furthermore, there are extraordinary pitfalls in the attempt. A person has only to try it to verify this. Therefore, the Zen Buddhist has had to turn his attention to aids for *zazen*. *Sanzen* and the work with koans are two such aids.[1]

As the zen student tries to sit quietly, to do *zazen*, he comes across all sorts of commonplace, yet curious obstructions to the activity. His nose itches and he wants to scratch it. He has to clear his throat. Difficulties like these keep appearing. Then he realizes that some of them can be controlled and others cannot. And he learns that it is not important to try to control those which cannot be controlled, those, for example, having to do with the involuntary nervous system. (Can a one-legged man become enlightened? He can't do *zazen*, really.) Then it becomes clear that he can control the others. This takes an effort of will, but it can be done. Rather easily he comes to be physically quiet for varying periods of time.

Other obstructions appear. His legs begin to ache. They go to sleep. And, if they do not, the muscles in his back or in his shoulders do. Then the instructor explains that there are exercises to help him with these problems. He tries them and they help, but not much. If he is a Westerner, he may think, "Perhaps if I did *zazen* in a chair it would be better." The instructor suggests that he try. He does, and he finds that it is just as hard physically to sit straight in a chair and do nothing for an hour as it is to sit cross-legged on the floor. So he goes back to the exercises, those other aids to *zazen*, and gradually things improve. He gets to the point where he can go through a two-hour *zazen* period without pain.

About this time the serious obstructions may appear. He has learned to sit quietly. He has even learned to be mentally quiet for short periods. Then it comes. "What the hell am I doing this for? So what, so you sit quietly. Meanwhile you look pretty damn silly sitting here day after day like an old fakir. Talk about being free. Talk about being enlightened. I'm just becoming a slave to another habit."

It is not that he cannot sit now. It is that somehow he does not want to. And this is part of not being able to sit. Something in him has to be cut out and controlled.

This is a sufficiently strong impediment to *zazen* that it nearly works. It nearly makes the student stop *zazen*. And it is here that the *hard* work starts. For it is here that something far harder to control than his body is asserting itself, namely, himself. Or his ego, as this "thing" is sometimes called. He is faced with the seemingly impossible, something like lifting himself by his own bootstraps.

Possibly in this connection or one like it, the use of the koan and the practice of *sanzen* came into existence. Koans are either anecdotes about Zen masters and their disciples or about two masters; or a koan may be a question about such an anecdote. It may also be simply a question. Further, there are what might be called major koans and minor or satellite koans that "cluster" about a major one.

One of the major koans is the *mu* koan. As is the case with most koans, it is an anecdote about which the student who is given it is asked a question, which is *his* koan; and the anecdote has a background that is provided for the student when he is given the koan. The background of the *mu* koan is this. The

Buddha said that all creatures have Buddha-nature. The anecdote is: One day a monk asked Joshu (an old teacher), Does the dog have Buddha-nature or not? Joshu replied: *Mu!* (which means, no). But how can that be? asked the monk; the Buddha said that all creatures have Buddha-nature. *Mu,* said Joshu. . . . The student who is given this koan is then asked: What does Joshu's *mu* mean? And the student may be told that he has to transcend the opposites of existence and non-existence to find the answer.

Sanzen is a private interview with the *roshi.* These interviews are short, and during intensive periods of study the zen student may have up to five of them a day. The basis for the interview is the koan or question on which the student is working. This question has been given to him to help him to cut through that part of himself that is now presenting the obstructions to his *zazen.*[2] As he works away with this sword, his hand often needs guiding. Hence the interview with the *roshi,* who, having learned to use the sword himself, is able to lend a helping hand and to enable the student to use his sword (i.e., his koan) more effectively.

When that sword has done its job and cut through that portion of his ego for which it is particularly useful, the student is given another.[3] And so it goes. For years, ten to an indefinite number, and with hundreds of koans the zen student hews away and seeks to improve his *zazen.*

The *mu* koan may serve feebly as an illustration here. I say "feebly" because nothing can successfully illustrate a process that has to be experienced to be appreciated; that is, which is living as well as intellectual. However, in a general way, here is what is involved. The serious obstructions to *zazen* come from the student himself, from his ego. So he is often given as his first koan Joshu's *mu*. '*Mu*' means no, or nothing, or emptiness. Working with this koan, the student is trying to "understand" this no, nothing, emptiness. He is striving, that is, to become empty himself—or egoless. The koan helps him in this (he is trying to understand *nothing*), and the *roshi* helps him as his ego fights back, leading him astray. The outcome is egolessness—or at least some, for this is only one koan and the affair is one of steps. The *mu* koan is, however, a major koan for it concerns the whole matter with which the student is grappling: the achievement of egolessness, the condition of enlightenment, the state in which no obstruction to *zazen* remains or, at least, has any effect.[4] For egolessness is not a negative condition. It is a positive one. The student is "egoless" when he can control his ego, when it does not, so to speak, make any difference.

The task is made even more difficult by the fact that the student is entirely on his own in this practice. The *roshi* can and will help him back to the path when he strays from it. He can do this because he himself has traversed that path. But the student has to do his own walking, he has to furnish the energy, and only he can remove the obstacles because they are in him

—another reason for saying that Zen cannot be transmitted in books.

You may well ask: Why indulge in the practice? Why struggle like this? Why perform these extraordinary labors? (And are these questions themselves not koans?) The zen student asks himself the same thing, and often it brings him to the point where he wants to quit. Or to the point where he will quit, a point at which his teachers will use physical force to make him continue—to have the *sanzen* interview with the *roshi,* for example.

The answers to these questions cannot be given to the student. However, each step forward, as he makes it, shows him why he indulges in the practice. And successive steps give him fresh evidence. For with each step forward he becomes stronger and freer. He has, for example, wanted to quit *sanzen,* to leave the temple compound forever. So tricky are the resistances to *zazen* that the act of leaving may even appear to him as the "answer" to his koan. He has been told that he will get the answer when he can transcend the opposites of existence and non-existence. Well, is not leaving the whole affair and going out into the world on his own transcending the opposites? It is certainly "getting beyond" the koan. Furthermore, he has read (and here is how books can fool him)—he has read of the independence of the enlightened man.

But then he takes a step forward, for logic will not do. He realizes that he does not *have* to do *sanzen.* He sees, too, that he does not *have* to quit it. He can take it or leave it. Months of *zazen* have produced a result. If he had left the temple at this time, *never* to return, he would not have been free. You are free when you can stay or go. So he returns to *sanzen*. And the strength that this move took is somehow not dissipated in the move. The zen student is stronger now.

After one of these steps he may understand some of the ritual employed as another aid to *zazen*, that is, to zen study. The zen student, for example, bows to the *roshi* when he enters the latter's room for *sanzen*. He bows when he leaves, down on his knees with his forehead touching the floor. He leaves with his hands cupped, to hold what the *roshi* has given him.[5] He bows to the cushions on which he practices his *zazen*, before *zazen* and after. All this seems senseless and ritualistic, formal. And it is, until the student sees one day that the bow to the cushion is a "thank you." The cushion is helping. It "deserves" a bow. The *roshi* deserves a bow. And *then* the student sees that he is bowing to himself when he is bowing to the cushion. Feelings of humbleness and dignity overwhelm him. He sees that the cushion is a part of it, the *roshi* is a part of it, he is a part of it. Of what? Of *zazen*.

The insight goes deeper. Parts of it? There are no parts. They are all one. The cushion deserves a bow, not "deserves" a bow. The distinction between the animate and the inanimate, the *roshi*, the student, and the cushion disappears. The student had thought that the cushion cannot, properly speaking, *deserve* anything. People deserve things; inanimate objects do not. People have purposes and make plans. Inanimate objects do not. That is right. But now the student has caught a glimpse of another way of looking at things, a way according to which there are no distinctions of this sort. For a moment he and the cushion are one. For a moment the *roshi* is not helping him; he is helping himself. In bowing to others, he is bowing to himself. And in bowing to himself, he is bowing to others. The bow is not a mere ritual. It is fraught with significance. It too is *zazen.*

This is not a manner of speaking and no more. Nor is it a theory. It describes an experience to which his *zazen* has led the student.

Even so, the seas of language can run high. Let's get out of the wind.

8

Satori

THERE has been so much talk of *satori* that Westerners have come to think of it as *SATORI!!* Actually, the closer one gets to Zen Buddhism the less he hears of *satori*. That is, as he moves from the literature on Zen to talking to people on the fringes of Zen Buddhism, to talking to Zen Buddhist monks, to talking to a *roshi,* the less he hears the word '*satori.*'

One day I asked an American disciple of Goto Roshi about this. The disciple had studied Zen for eight years. He laughed at my question. Then he told me that when he had been with the *roshi* for six years he had asked the same question. The *roshi* replied to this effect:

We do not worry about *satori* or getting it, whatever it may be. If you suddenly see a thing as you have not seen it before, a little more clearly perhaps, or if you suddenly feel contact with a person, and credit these experiences to your *zazen* and your work with the koans, that is all right. We call these experiences by-products of the process. But do not aim for them. We do not aim for them. And you may progress without them.

Hakuin (1685–1768) was one of the great Japanese Zen Buddhist teachers. He also devised a koan called the one-hand koan. Two hands brought smartly together make a clapping noise. What is the sound of one hand? It is a fine koan for appreciating the difficulties of zen study.

Hakuin wrote an autobiography and other works in which he related his experiences with Zen study, for example, the experience of "solving" a koan. In one of these books, the *Orategama,* he reports that he had later and deeper mystical experiences after he "solved" his first koan, some of which came with reading verse. He also talks of six or seven great enlightenments (awakenings) and innumerable small ones that he got from hearing the snow fall and from other experiences of nature. One of these mystical experiences started as a dream from which he was awakened. In another he saw answers to all the koans with which he had worked different from those he had seen before. One of the greatest of these experiences came when he was forty-two while reading the *Lotus Sutra*. At that time, he reports, he saw the error of all his greater and lesser awakenings.

Rinzai Zen Buddhism is sometimes called ladder Zen. In the study, one moves up step by step. In the other metaphor: *zazen* is like an onion, though harder to get through.

It might be mentioned, finally, that the word *'satori'* is used in a variety of ways. It is sometimes used as though it referred to one of the steps that characterize zen study and progress in zen study. It is also used to refer to the final condition of enlightenment, which is said to lie at the end of zen study, a condition more often called *samadhi* (though *'samadhi'* itself is variously used). *'Satori'* is used to refer to a certain attitude toward life, the Buddhist. It is used to refer to the apprehending of a spiritual truth and to understanding Zen. It is used for intuitive perception of reality and for seeing into one's own nature. And it is used in English as though it referred to such intense psychological phenomena as those, for example, experienced by people after severe operations who, when they first eat, may find even in hospital food qualities that are "out of this world."

This latter usage has given rise to confusion. In fact *zazen* is not practiced to develop extraordinary powers or to produce magical effects. It is practiced solely to become quiet. Psychologists have supposed that the results achieved in *zazen* can be duplicated by taking drugs like mescaline. This notion misses the whole point of *zazen* and confuses *satori* with illusions and certain peculiar phenomena of perception. The latter can be induced by drugs, thus showing that drugs have nothing to do with mysticism. In the main, only hard work does.

Otherwise it is true that insight is important in zen study. Mere sitting is not it. A child, for example, is not doing *zazen* when he sits quietly, even with his legs crossed. *Zazen* is sitting with *awareness* that sitting *is* it.

"When Bankei was preaching at Ryumon temple, a Shinshu priest, who believed in salvation through the repetition of the name of the Buddha of Love, was jealous of his large audience and wanted to debate with him.

"Bankei was in the midst of a talk when the priest appeared, but the fellow made such a disturbance that Bankei stopped his discourse and asked about the noise.

" 'The founder of our sect,' boasted the priest, 'had such miraculous powers that he held a brush in his hand on one bank of the river, his attendant held up a paper on the other bank, and the teacher wrote the holy name of Amida through the air. Can you do such a wonderful thing?'

"Bankei replied lightly: 'Perhaps your fox can perform that trick, but that is not the manner of Zen. My miracle is that when I feel hungry I eat, and when I feel thirsty I drink.' " [1]

9

Other aids for zazen

IN the matter of the rituals that the zen student performs, be he layman or monk, there is a story of an American visiting a Zen Buddhist temple compound. (I say "compound" because there are not, strictly speaking, large Zen temples. A large Zen Buddhist "temple" is actually a group of buildings, each of which serves some purpose.) The American was being shown about by the abbot of the temple. The visitor noticed that the abbot was bowing to the various statues of the Bodhisattvas in the different buildings as they entered. Finally, in some annoyance he said to the abbot: "I thought that you were a Zen Buddhist and free of all this bowing and scraping. Hell, *I'm* freer than you. I can spit on these statues."

"Okay," replied the abbot in his limited English, "You spits, I bows." [1]

This story is true. It is like a koan. An awareness of such stories can help a student with his *zazen*. There follow some other sayings that perform this function. These other aids are not koans. They come in the form of little talks with the *roshi* at off moments during the day. In these talks the student may be presented with a piece of imagery, which helps him to concentrate in *zazen* by showing him in a concrete and practical way what he is striving for, which is also concrete and practical. The reader will remember the triangle and the *Daruma* doll in this connection.

One morning Goto Roshi spoke of his health, which was poor. He was eighty years old. He went on to say how well a certain person was caring for him. But she is not doing it for me, he said. She is doing it for my students. She tells me that my body is old and worn out, and she is right. But I must go on teaching so I obey her. That is Zen, knowing when to say "yes" and when to say "no," when to kill and when to give life, when you have to do this and when you have to do that. You must be pliant and elastic. . . . Then he talked of Aristotle's doctrine of the mean, although Aristotle's name was not mentioned.

The *roshi* continued: You, *you,* must be like an iron ball. Firm, yet able to roll anywhere with your center always at your center. Remember the triangle. Do not be top-heavy. Do not waver. Manjusri's sword (Manjusri is the Bodhisattva of Intuitive Wisdom. He is always depicted with a sword in hand.)— Manjusri's sword is for killing and for giving life. It kills illusions and gives strength. So must I, your *roshi,* at times kill you in order to give you life.

The *roshi* went on to compare his work to that of a carpenter who makes a column from a block of wood. First he knocks off the four edges, then he knocks off the edges that have resulted, and so on until he has the column.[2]

During another conversation, the *roshi* spoke of ancestors. You had two parents, they each had two, and so on. When you have gone back a hundred generations in this way, you see that an enormous number of people were involved in your birth. In a sense you are extraordinarily important. A tremendous amount of energy went into producing you. Yet now you are all that counts. Think of that effort, of all those people, when you are doing *zazen.* The effort and the people are all behind you. Get them behind you in *zazen.*

At another time, the *roshi* again alluded to ancestors. You are important, he said; you right here and now in this present moment in this room. But the other day you went to Osaka. It is worth reflecting on all that made that possible. The men who made the train, the men who ran it, the men who made your clothes, the station masters, the ticket sellers. There is even more to it than this. Your trip to Japan, the food you eat, everything that you do. Think how many people are involved in all this. Think about these things sometimes when you are doing *zazen*.

On another occasion, mention was made of a man who had achieved notoriety and who had recently suffered a stroke. Of him the *roshi* said: A plant that bears fruit does not aspire to go higher. Instead it bends gracefully under its load and is not noticed because of its high head. Only those who are not bearing fruit seek to go higher. Or, as the Buddhist says, only those who are not piling up virtue strive to go higher. Then they may have strokes. Lead a simple, quiet life and give your virtue to your students. Do not use it yourself. That is to be selfish. And anyway, what need have you of it when you are the sort of man who has borne fruit?

The *roshi* was using the word 'virtue' much as it is used by Spinoza, in the sense of strength.

One time several students were present. The subject of the weather came up. Of one of the students the *roshi* said that some of this person's days were nice and some were not. So it is with *zazen*, he said. Why do you ask me why it goes well at times and poorly at others? Where is the difference?

Once during work with his koan a student was troubled and felt severe frustration. He wanted to talk to the *roshi*, as man to man, so to speak. But the *roshi* would not.

We do not talk about *sanzen*, he said. I can see the trouble in your eyes; you do not have to tell me that you are troubled. But you have to do this on your own. It is a spiritual matter. And you have to come to an attitude, deep down inside. To talk about it lessens the chance that you will achieve it. You have to overcome what you feel now by yourself. Make an effort of will. Furthermore, I will not descend to talk to you. You must ascend to talk to me. It is the process that counts. People always get eager and rush ahead for the answer to the koan. But it is the spiritual process that counts. You cannot rush that. This is not something new that you are experiencing today. Others have been through it.[3]

Then it came out that the student's legs were hurting during *zazen*. The *roshi* rose and demonstrated some exercises that would loosen the muscles in the buttocks and back. They are causing the trouble, he said, not the thigh muscles, which are the ones that actually hurt.

He spoke again of the need to be pliable and flexible. Iron, for example, goes through three stages of curing. After the first two, it is brittle and will break when bent. Finally it gets "strong" and elastic and can be bent and spring back into shape. That has to be the condition of your body. Only then will you have a mind like that.[4]

During another conversation, the *roshi* remarked that a good description of zen study in the language of the West is the old dictum: Know thyself. That is all that you are trying to do now, he said.

It is important to add, parenthetically, that there are two quite different meanings of the word 'know.' There is the meaning that occurs in statements like 'I know that bodies fall with a certain rate of acceleration.' And there is the meaning that occurs in statements like 'Abraham knew Sara and she was with child.' The first kind of knowing is conceptual, the second direct. Dictionaries define the second kind as carnal knowledge, which is almost inextricably linked in our minds with sexual intercourse. Break the linkage for a moment, however, and reflect on *carnal* knowledge. It is bodily knowledge. And then think of *zazen* and how in it one becomes aware of the body. Then of his thoughts. Then of his deepest thoughts.

Having said that zen study is knowing yourself, the *roshi* went on: In America you have democracy, which means for you government of the people, by the people, and for the people. I in my turn am bringing democracy to Japan. You cannot have democracy until people know themselves. The Chinese said that government is unnecessary and they were right. When people know themselves and have their own strength, they do not need government. Otherwise they are just a mob and must be ruled. On the other hand, when the rulers do not know themselves, they push the people around. When you do not know yourself, you busy yourself with other people. Zen study is just a matter of getting your own feet on the ground.

Another time, the *roshi* spoke of a deep ocean of tranquillity, completely calm. The zen student is striving to penetrate to that calm, he said.

We know all this, one wants to say; much of it is in the teachings of the West. This is true. Mr. Blyth has pointed out in *Zen in English Literature and Oriental Classics* that portions of Western literature are full of Zen. However, they are not full of references to a practice like *zazen*. And even when *zazen* is mentioned in books about Zen, it is glossed over in favor of talk of the philosophy of Zen. Then the *use* to which even that is put by the Buddhist is overlooked, for when a *roshi* talks philosophy he does so to improve his pupils' *zazen*. He is not interested in philosophy *per se*. Goto Roshi, for example, discussed the philosophy of democracy. He did so, however, in order to bring out the practical bearings of *zazen*. This can help a zen student with his *zazen* by making him realize that it is not *outré*. The idea that *zazen* will result in supernatural experience is an impediment to its successful practice.

10

Zazen overlooked

IN Buddhist literature, as distinct from literature about Buddhism, the metaphor of "the other shore" appears frequently. Enlightenment or the condition of freedom is often described as being on the other shore. The root of the metaphor is also used in a common simile, which makes a crucial point when it is carefully listened to. The teachings of the Buddha are likened to a raft, which is used to cross to the other shore. And of these teachings it is said that one abandons them when one is on the other shore. Just as one would leave a raft with which he had crossed a river and not dream of taking it with him.

Fortunately or unfortunately, the practice of *zazen* is an affair of steps. With each of these steps the zen student gets to another shore. The description of Zen Buddhism as "sudden enlightenment" Buddhism has obscured this progression, although it is true in its way. For it easily leads a person to think of "the other shore" as absolutely another shore and only as an absolutely other shore.

After the student has taken the one step into *zazen,* the step from the study of Zen to zen study, from the books to the practice, it is interesting to look back through the books and note how this step has been neglected and how obscure it is when it is mentioned.

Here are a few examples. In a selection from the writings of D. T. Suzuki called *Zen Buddhism,* edited by William Barrett, there are chapters on the meaning of Zen, its historical background, *satori,* and the doctrine of no-mind, but none on *zazen.* There is even a chapter called "Practical Methods of Zen Instruction," which contains no mention of *zazen,* although the editor defines 'Zen' in his Introduction as 'meditation' and refers to *dhyana.*

Then there is R. H. Blyth's delightful book *Zen in English Literature and Oriental Classics.* In his Preface, Blyth succinctly defines Zen both as "a religious system, that is, a certain way of thinking about life; and living in accord with reality." He clearly favors the latter. However, Blyth nowhere in the book mentions *zazen* despite the fact that he is intimately acquainted with Zen Buddhism and is not merely a student of it. Moreover, the description of Don Quixote as the perfect example of the man who lives by Zen ignores *zazen* as Quixote did not practice it.

In person Blyth is as delightful as his works, but he does not tell us in his books how he became so Zen Buddhist. Yet, if you visit him in Tokyo, he will tell you that you "really must practice Zen (meditation) in a *zendo*.[1] It is an essential experience if you want to know about Zen."

There is also available now a translation of *On the Transmission of Mind,* called *The Zen Teaching of Huang Po.* In his Introduction the translator, Mr. John Blofeld, informs the reader that there is very little in the book about the practice of meditation. He indicates that Huang Po apparently assumed that his audience knew about it. Although this section of the Introduction is entitled "Dhyana Practice," Mr. Blofeld drops the matter there and completes the section with a discussion of enlightenment or the *outcome* of the practice.

This neglect of *zazen* is not universal in the writings of Zen Buddhists and those who write about Zen Buddhism, although it is universal among those writers who have had no contact with Zen except through books. Indeed, *zazen* is both mentioned and described by most of those who have practiced it and then gone on to write or to talk about Zen Buddhism. Mr. Suzuki has an excellent book called *The Training of the Zen Buddhist Monk,* in which by far the longest of the six chapters is concerned with meditation or *zazen*. However, it was printed in an edition of only 500 copies and privately circulated by Suzuki to libraries, so that it has not been widely read. It now may receive more attention, however, because it was reprinted in 1960.

Furthermore, one of the best books on Zen Buddhism and the only one in English written by a Zen *roshi* devotes considerable space to the practice of *dhyana*. This is *Sermons of a Buddhist Abbot* by Soyen Shaku. It was published by Open Court in 1906, in the days before the word 'Zen' automatically appeared in the title of any book about Zen Buddhism. But it has long been out of print.

When one's purpose, then, is to call attention to *zazen,* it is worth asking why the practice of Zen has been neglected in the books on Zen Buddhism and why it is so obscure in them when it is mentioned. Not only does some awareness of these matters call more attention to the practice of Zen, but it may also help to take some of the mystery out of Zen Buddhism and reduce the mystique that has grown up about it. For example, Barrett in his Introduction to the selections from Suzuki makes much of the non-conceptual aspect of Zen and then proceeds to make a mystery of this by never more than mentioning the *practice,* which, together with the aids for it, is as much as anything the non-conceptual aspect of Zen.

There are, I suppose, many reasons for the obscurity in which *zazen* has lain and for the consequent obfuscation of Zen Buddhism, which is no more mysterious, although it is far more difficult, than sawing wood. A few of these are set forth below and in the succeeding chapter.

First, even when it is clearly stated that meditation is at the heart of Zen Buddhism and that Zen Buddhism is Meditation Buddhism, the matter does not become clear to a Westerner. For the word 'meditation' does not mean *zazen*. It means something quite different. Thus the translation of the word 'Zen' is at the same time a help and a hindrance in furthering the understanding of Zen Buddhism. It calls attention to the essence of the thing only to hide it in an ambiguity in the word 'meditation,' which is created by the very act of translation.

There is, second, the fact that the practice of *zazen* is as familiar in the Orient as it is unfamiliar in the Occident. As Suzuki remarked: ". . . the Buddha lived among people who were trained in all sorts of concentration called *samadhi*." [2] And some practice of meditation has been common in the East ever since. This results in two other factors. On the one hand, because he is so accustomed to it and because he does not realize that the Westerner is not, the Oriental interpreter of Zen Buddhism does not see the need for stressing *zazen* for his Western listeners. On the other hand, precisely because it is quite unfamiliar to him, the Westerner does not appreciate the importance of *zazen* even when he does read about it.

Connected with the foregoing is the fact that philosophy is

so much a matter of thinking and of words for the Westerner. This makes him slight the mention of a physical practice *in connection with philosophy,* though he does not elsewhere. He knows full well that you do not learn to swim by reading a book and avoiding the water, even though a book may help. The same factor works to deceive the Oriental. In the atmosphere of the West, he loses sight of his own practice and comes to stress what it appears that the Westerner wants: the high-sounding words which can go with that practice.

There are also the facts that *zazen* is hard work and that the Westerner, in his philosophizing, tends to be lazy. Or, if not lazy, he tends to abstractions and an avoidance of the concrete, of which hard work is a part.

All these factors also work to deepen another obscurity, which is closely related to that which surrounds *zazen* and which throws the latter even more into the dark. This is the shadow on the notion of enlightenment or sudden awakening that forms in the Westerner's mind as he reads about Zen. It appears to him inevitably as an intellectual phenomenon. That it is a matter of the body as well as of the mind does not easily occur to him. And even when it does, if the occurrence comes without the physical practices of enlightenment, it does not mean much. This is abetted by the talk of *sudden* enlightenment, which makes it appear that nothing has to be done or can be done to obtain enlightenment, that it just comes. This impression is strengthened by a host of Zen stories concerning so and so getting enlightenment when he heard a bell and such and such getting it when he heard a tile strike a tree. The impression has been further strengthened by the omission in most of these stories of the facts that so and so was at the time assiduously practicing *zazen,* that such and such had been practicing it for ten years, and that both went right on practicing it after the lightning struck.

It might finally be mentioned that some sort of dualism is endemic in Western thought. It may be in Eastern thought too, but if so it would not have the influence of obscuring *zazen* for the Westerner that Western dualism does. There are, for examples, the dualisms of the flesh and the spirit, of God and the world, of man and nature, the Platonic dualism of the real world and the world of becoming, and the Cartesian dualism of mind and matter. This latter is the more recent and for the intellectual probably the most influential, at least as far as his reading and thinking go. Even when the Westerner tends to some form of monism in his philosophy, in materialism, for example, it is still a philosophy and, hence, a thing of the mind. Small wonder, then, that the practice of Zen as a *physical* as well as a mental affair should escape him. He is aware of physical practices, and of mental ones, but his philosophy tends to make it impossible for him to appreciate a practice that is both.

There are, however, these stories:

[1]   "NAN-IN, a Japanese master during the Meiji era (1868–1912), received a university professor who came to inquire about Zen.

"Nan-in served tea. He poured his visitor's cup full, and then kept on pouring.

"The professor watched until he no longer could restrain himself. 'It is overfull. No more will go in!'

" 'Like this cup,' Nan-in said, 'you are full of your own opinions and speculations. How can I show you Zen unless you first empty your cup?' "

[2]   THE following is told of Hui-neng, a famous early teacher of Zen Buddhism in China.

"He saw some monks arguing about a fluttering pennant; one of them said, 'The pennant is an inanimate object and it is the wind that makes it flap.' Against this it was remarked by another monk that 'Both wind and pennant are inanimate things, and the flapping is an impossibility.' A third one protested, 'The flapping is due to a certain combination of cause and condition'; while a fourth one proposed a theory, saying, 'After all there is no flapping pennant, but it is the wind that is moving by itself.' The discussion grew quite animated when Hui-neng interrupted with the remark, 'It is neither wind nor pennant but your own mind which flaps.' This at once put a stop to the heated argument." [3]

58

11

Zazen, not quietism

ZEN Buddhism has been described as the religion of tranquillity. This is a good description but, like so many brief statements, it is misleading; for it encourages the charges that the practice of *zazen* is a quietistic practice and that it leads to retirement from the world.

The person who tries *zazen* soon sees through the first charge. He finds that it takes enormous activity of a certain kind to prevent his mind from racing along as he sits. Even the beginner who has been instructed to concentrate on his breathing discovers that he is lucky if he gets to the count of three before he is off on a train of thought. Later when he is working with a koan and even though he has now had some practice in sitting, the zen student is aware of this phenomenon. Both the beginner and the more advanced student appreciate the Zen description of our ordinary minds as "monkey minds." They are so busy that one wonders that the noise they make is not audible to others. There is no quietism in the overcoming of this busyness and in the rigorous use of counting and then koans in the struggle.[1]

However, the impression that Zen Buddhism is quietism is and has been so strong even in the Orient that some of the developments in its history have been moves to counteract this impression. The matter has not been improved by the fact that there are tendencies on the part of those who come to Zen to slide into mere quietism. On the one hand, unless the student is mightily determined and unless he works assiduously with his practice, he can come merely to sit. The effort may prove too much. On the other hand, even if he makes considerable progress, he may still get stuck in what is called the Zen cave and fail to take the next step out of it. That is, he may come to prefer the school to the world for which it is the school, the monastic life to the hectic workaday world. This is one of the obstructions to *zazen,* and it is a pitfall from which only extraordinary work on his part and that of his teacher can extricate him.[2]

The charge of quietism and the foregoing tendencies bring out another reason why *zazen* has been overlooked in Western literature about Zen Buddhism. Although that literature is now fairly large, it is dominated by the work of Professor Suzuki, who is by far the most influential interpreter of Zen for the West. Of the more than a dozen of his books, his three volumes entitled *Essays in Zen Buddhism* form the core of his writings. And they have obscured the importance of *zazen*.

This fact is mainly due to Suzuki's concern throughout the series to combat both the charge of and the tendency to quietism. For this reason he has stressed those aspects of the history of Zen Buddhism that deal with efforts and the development of techniques for the combating of quietism; and he has stressed the aspect of insight or intuitive understanding in the practice of the Zen Buddhist to show that his practice is anything but mere sitting when it is properly carried out.

However, he has stressed the matter of insight so greatly that, as far as Western readers are concerned, the pendulum has swung in the other direction and the importance of *zazen* has been overlooked.

Thus, if one turns to the indices in Suzuki's books, one finds very few references to *zazen* or to meditation. One also finds only some thirty pages out of more than one thousand devoted to explicit discussion of *zazen*. And in a chapter on the *zendo* or meditation hall in the first volume, there is no mention of what the hall is primarily used for. Furthermore, there are dozens of the stories, to which allusion has already been made, of how this or that man became enlightened by something that a master said or did, perhaps a single word or a blow; and yet there are few references to the facts that all of those who became enlightened were at the time practicing *zazen,* that they continued to do so after the insight came to them, and that they got further insights.

The result of this stress for the unknowing reader has been the impression that the insights are what count and that these come about solely because of some tricky saying or violent action by a MASTER. Indeed, in the long chapter called "Practical Methods of Zen Instruction," these verbal tricks are discussed at length and classified, giving him who is not aware that they presuppose *zazen* the idea that short lectures, pithy remarks, and blows are the only methods of Zen instruction. In actuality, they are preceded by instruction in *zazen* and are accompanied by the constant and unremitting practice of it.

In sum, *zazen* has been neglected by the Western interest in Zen partly because the leading interpreter of Zen has been concerned in so much of that interpretation with refuting the charge of quietism.

However, Suzuki has not been guilty of omission. For the zen student, the references in *Essays in Zen Buddhism* to *zazen* are there, even though most of them are implicit and thus likely to be overlooked by one who is not doing *zazen. Zazen* forms the background for most of the three volumes. It is only an obscure background because Suzuki is so concerned to bring out the point that *zazen* is not mere sitting, that it is sitting which is accompanied by enormous activity of a certain kind.[3]

That *zazen* does not eventuate in retreat from the world when practiced assiduously is attested not only by innumerable references by Zen teachers to the student's "everyday life" but also by the custom in Zen temples that requires everyone to work. There is an old saying among Zen Buddhists that a day of no work is a day of no eating.[4]

Entertaining evidence in this direction is a series of ancient pictures which have appeared in various reproductions. These are the ten cow-herding pictures in which are depicted stages through which the zen student progresses in his movement toward enlightenment or freedom. These pictures are to be found in Suzuki's first volume of essays, as well as in *Zen Flesh and Zen Bones* and other books.

Possibly because the cow has been a sacred animal in India it has had a prominent place in Buddhist literature, where it has appeared in parables for illuminating men's spiritual lives. One of these stories, which Suzuki reports, is particularly apt in relation to the ten cow-herding pictures. Tai-an asked Pai-chang, "I wish to know about the Buddha; what is he?" Pai-chang answered, "It is like seeking for an ox while you yourself are on it." "What shall I do after I know?" "It is like going home riding on it." "How do I look after it all the time in order to be in accordance with (the way)?" The master then told him, "You should behave like the cow-herd, who, carrying a staff, sees to it that his cattle won't wander away into some-one else's rice fields."

In the first of the cow-herding pictures, a man with a halter is shown in the fields looking for the cow. In the next picture, he comes upon traces of it (as though a man were to read of Zen or the good life in a book). In the third picture, the man sees the cow ahead of him on a path, partly obscured by a tree. In the following picture, he throws his halter and catches the cow (as though the reader of the book were now working at *zazen*). Next he is shown leading it, or perhaps taming it, for the cow appears to long for the sweet grasses. In the sixth picture, we find him heading for home on the cow's back. Is he, as Suzuki suggests, humming a tune? At home, in the seventh picture, the cow is forgotten and the man is sitting alone. Is he going to forsake the world? In the following pic-ture, both the cow and the man have disappeared. There is only a circle with nothing in it. Complete serenity. The ninth picture depicts a scene in nature, a low, wooded hill. It is as though the man has gone back to the source for he does not appear in the picture. But that is not all, for there is the tenth and last picture. In it the man is seen entering the city, carry-ing a sack and a basket. He is bare-chested and smiling. In the text and poem that often accompany each of these pictures, it is said of the tenth:

"Entering the City with Bliss-bestowing Hands. His humble cottage door is closed, and the wisest know him not. No glimpses of his inner life are to be caught; for he goes on his own way without following the steps of the ancient sages. Carrying a gourd he goes out into the market; leaning against a stick he comes home. He is found in the company with wine-bibbers and butchers; he and they are all converted into Buddhas.

"Barechested and barefooted, he comes into the marketplace;
Daubed with mud and ashes how broadly he smiles!
There is no need for the miraculous power of the gods,
For he touches, and lo! The dead trees come into full bloom." [5]

12

The vigor in zazen

IT might be said that the zen student is striving for quietness in action. The quietness, however, is full of vigor. This may be observed in a Zen Buddhist. It also appears in the records that have been kept of the teachings of the old masters. Until recently only two of these records were available in English. One is the record of Huang Po called *On the Transmission of Mind*. The other is the *Sutra of Hui-Neng* (published by Luzac and Co., London). Now, however, a number of others have appeared in a three-volume collection of translations by Lu K'uan Yü (Charles Luk) called *Ch'an and Zen Teaching*. Because these records are interesting reading as well as demonstrations of the vigor in Zen, there follow some excerpts from the *Rinzai Record*.[1]

(a) Rinzai ascended to his seat (i.e., the teacher's raised seat) in the hall and a monk came forward. Rinzai gave a "Ho!" The monk also shouted, and then bowed. Whereupon Rinzai hit him with his stick.

Commentary: Since the monk came forward to ask a question, Rinzai shouted to quell his thinking and thus help him toward enlightenment. The monk failed by not leaving immediately after bowing. Had he done so he would have revealed a degree of enlightenment.[2]

(b) Joshu on a trip came to Rinzai's monastery. While he was washing his feet in the yard, Rinzai saw him and asked: "Why did Bodhidharma come from the West?"

Joshu replied: "The matter was like this mountain monk washing his feet."

Rinzai approached the visitor as though he were listening for something. Joshu said: "You understand all this. What's the use of fishing from others?" Thereupon Rinzai returned to the abbot's room.

Joshu: "Although I have been working for thirty years, I did poorly today."

Commentary: Joshu was the Zen master widely known for his *mu* koan. Rinzai was probing Joshu, who immediately exposed the trick. As Joshu also proved to be a Zen expert, Rinzai had nothing further to say and returned to his room. This

68

showed his enlightenment. Joshu observed that he had given by mistake a correct interpretation to one who knew it already.[3]

(c) Rinzai asked a monk: "Where do you come from?" The monk replied: "From Ting Chou." Rinzai reached for his staff. The monk wondered whether he should add anything. Thereupon Rinzai gave him a blow. When the monk remonstrated with Rinzai, the latter said: "Someday you will meet a man who understands this."

Later the monk related the incident to San Sheng who immediately hit him and, as the latter thought of a response, hit him again.

Commentary: Rinzai reached for his staff to test the monk. When the latter bethought himself of something to say, Rinzai hit him.

San Sheng was Rinzai's disciple. He gave the monk two blows to quiet his disturbed mind and to help him to enlightenment.[4]

(d) On his way to visit Feng Lin Rinzai met an old woman who asked him where he was going. "To Feng Lin's," he replied. "Feng Lin is out," said the woman. When Rinzai asked: "Where did he go?", the woman went off without answering. Rinzai called: "Hoi!" When the woman looked back, Rinzai continued his journey.

Commentary: The woman did not understand Zen very well. Up to the moment when she left without replying to Rinzai's question she was on the right track. However, when Rinzai called to test her, she failed by looking back. Rinzai continued his journey, sure that he would find Feng Lin.

(e) Rinzai was on his raised seat in the hall. Ma Ku asked: "That statue of a Bodhisattva has twelve faces, which face is the right one?" Rinzai descended, grabbed Ma Ku and said: "Where has the Bodhisattva gone? Speak! Speak!" Ma Ku turned to ascend to the seat and Rinzai raised his stick to hit him. Ma Ku took hold of the stick and together they went to Rinzai's room.

Commentary: Ma Ku was also a master. His question tested Rinzai. Rinzai's actions were his reply. The subsequent actions showed each master's enlightenment. They departed in understanding.[5]

(f) Rinzai asked a visiting nun: "Is your coming good or evil?" Nun: "Ho!" Rinzai lifted his stick and said: "Speak again! Speak again!" Nun: "Ho!" Rinzai struck her.

Commentary: The first shout by the nun was correct. The second was repetitious and showed inflexibility. So Rinzai hit her.

(g) Once again Rinzai was on his raised seat. Ma Ku asked him: "That statue of the Bodhisattva has a thousand eyes on his thousand hands, which eye is the right one?" Rinzai grabbed Ma Ku and repeated the question, then: "Speak! Speak!" Ma Ku pulled Rinzai down and took the seat himself. Rinzai: "How are you doing?" Ma Ku hesitated. Whereupon Rinzai shouted: "Ho!" and pulled Ma Ku from the seat. Ma Ku left the hall.

Commentary: Ma Ku's act of pulling Rinzai from the seat was correct. Then Rinzai changed his tactics, throwing Ma Ku into confusion. However, Ma Ku finally leaves the hall, showing that he has understood.[6]

(h) A monk: "What is the essence of Buddhism?" Rinzai raised his stick. The monk: "Ho!" Rinzai hit him.

Another monk asked Rinzai: "What is the essence of Buddhism?" Again Rinzai raised his stick. The monk: "Ho!" Rinzai: "Ho!" The monk hesitated. Whereupon Rinzai hit him.

Rinzai then addressed the assembly: "One should be ready to lose his soul for the Dharma. When I was with my teacher, Huang Po, I asked him three times about the essence of Buddhism and thrice he beat me till I shook. Who can repeat this experience for me?"

A monk: "I can." Rinzai extended his staff. The monk reached for it, but received a blow instead.

Commentary: The first monk's 'Ho' was weak, so Rinzai struck him. Rinzai was more lenient with the second monk, but the latter's hesitation earned him a blow. The third monk was caught in Rinzai's trap and received a blow to teach him awareness of Rinzai and of himself instead of concern with an illusory stick.[7]

(i) Rinzai went with P'u Hua (the assembly leader) to the

home of a patron of the monastery. While they were eating dinner Rinzai asked the leader: "Does the sentence 'A hair can contain the great ocean and a mustard seed Mount Sumeru' display the Buddha's great powers or are these things self-evident?" P'u Hua sprang to his feet, and upset the table. Rinzai: "Too coarse!" P'u Hua: "Is this a place where you can talk of coarseness and refinement?"

Commentary: Rinzai set a trap for P'u Hua by quoting the Buddha's saying about the ocean and Mount Sumeru. The saying expresses metaphorically what the mind can accomplish when enlightened. Rinzai was testing P'u Hua's enlightenment. The latter met the test with an action instead of a discussion which would show that he was caught up in ideas.

Zen Buddhists regard an enlightened mind as a holy site. Thus, when Rinzai countered by accusing P'u Hua of being unmannerly, P'u Hua replied that they were in a place (the home of the patron, a holy site) where there can be neither coarseness nor refinement, that is, no dualism. Once again he showed his enlightenment.

(j) The following day they were again at meal. Rinzai asked P'u Hua: "Is today's offering the same as yesterday's?" P'u Hua again overturned the table. Rinzai: "Although your act is correct, it is too coarse." P'u Hua: "Ho! You blind fool! Does a Buddha talk about coarseness and refinement?" Rinzai stuck out his tongue.

Commentary: Once more Rinzai tests P'u Hua. Would he discriminate and make a comparison between two meals? P'u Hua replies with his great gesture, wiping out all traces of discrimination. Rinzai concedes that he is right, and makes another probe. P'u Hua shouts to reveal his true self. It cannot be deceived. His question then confirms his enlightenment. Rinzai puts out his tongue to express his amazement at P'u Hua's achievement.

(k) Officer Wang of the imperial guard once went with Rinzai to the monks' hall. Wang: "Do the monks read sutras in this hall?" Rinzai: "No." Wang: "Do they undergo Zen training?" Rinzai: "No." Wang: "If they do neither, what do they do?" Rinzai: "They are taught to become Buddhas and Patriarchs." Wang: "Although gold powder is dear, it will blind the eyes when thrown into them." Rinzai: "I thought you were only a worldly man."

Commentary: Wang knew something about Zen, for he said that if one clung to sutras and meditation he would be blinded —using the metaphor of the gold powder and the eyes.[8]

13

From sayings of Rinzai

I HAVE no teaching. All I can do for you is to cure your illnesses and release your minds from the fetters that bind them.

Don't cling to my words. Rather, stop thinking and trying to find the answers. And do it now!

If you understand, you will fear neither birth nor death. You will be free to stay or leave.

Don't seek Buddhahood, for it will come to you when least expected.

Don't be deceived by others. Trust yourself. That is all that is required.

If you lack faith in yourself, you will cling to externals and lose your freedom.

You have no faith in yourself. So you look for something without. Even if you succeed you will have only names and words. You will not have the living principle.

In all the variety of our daily activities is there anything lacking? All is there, and he who is able to perceive it can live his life without care.

Seek nothing from without. Then you are a Buddha.

The scholars and sutras! I spit on them! You have only to know that wherever you are you are on the road to your own home.

It is only because our wisdom is screened by our feelings and our substance changed by our thoughts that we endure suffering.

I tell you, there is nothing which is not important nor a living being who cannot be liberated.

When you come to see things as I do, you can sit on the heads of the Buddhas.

The hope of enlightenment is like a yoke about your neck. Buddhahood is the filth in the latrine.

Bodhidharma and *Nirvana* are hitching posts for asses. Forget all this stuff.

Don't worry. Take things as they are. Walk when you want to walk. Sit when you want to sit.

If you seek the Buddha, he will become a mere name.

Time is precious.

Don't copy those who busy themselves with studies of Zen, learning names and sayings.

Be simple; cast off rigid customs and habits.

Without faith in yourself you recognize only names and words. You fools! You try to find in books what your deluded minds want.

Cherish neither the sacred nor the secular.

Don't practice and strive. Just be simple and unconcerned in all your doings, whether they be wearing clothes, eating, defecating, or making water.

Those who strive for success are stupid.

Nowadays students of Zen are like goats. They will eat anything, taking even garbage for nourishment. The blind fools!

Doubt is a demon. A Buddha knows that nothing has been created, that there is nothing to lose or to gain, nothing to realize.

There is no cause for wondering. But because you do not believe this your every thought is directed to the pursuit of externals. You are like a man who rejects his own head to look for another.

The real is ready at hand and does not wait for an opportune time.

There is no fixed teaching. All I can provide is an appropriate medicine for a particular ailment.

Don't turn to the masters of old, thinking: there's the truth. They are crutches for idiots.

Buddhahood comes from freedom from reliance. But it is itself no gain. He who doesn't understand this is beset by doctrines which only blind him.

If you want to be independent, free from birth and death, recognize yourself.

The enlightened man turns his back on the scriptures. They are but steps to enlightenment.

Time is precious. There is no permanence in an instant. (Change is ceaseless.)

If you give rise to a thought of love, you will be drowned. If you give rise to a thought of anger, you will be burned. If you give rise to a thought of doubt, you will be bound. If you give rise to a thought of joy, you will be torn by the wind.

Nothing is objectionable. If you despise the secular and prize the sacred, you are in bondage to the secular and to the sacred.

Followers of the Way, make no mistake. Nothing has a nature of its own [an essence]—though names delude us in this.

What do you seek? Even the greatest teachings are but waste paper, good for cleaning up a mess.

All longing produces suffering.

Why do you take the Buddha to be the ultimate? Didn't he die too? How do I differ from him?

Following others and succeeding in bookish learning will leave you in chains. It is far better to forget the big questions and to go to some quiet place to meditate. But that takes work!

What is there to doubt!

Let go. Don't seek or run away.

Make no mistake, there's nothing to be found without or within. And don't hang on to my words. Go your way in calm and with an empty mind. It is enough to be quiet and ordinary, wearing your robe and eating your rice.

All afflictions have their source in the mind. Why seek elsewhere to be rid of them?

If you meet a Buddha, cut him down! If you meet a Patriarch, cut him down! Your parents? Cut them down! Your relatives? Cut them down! Only thus will you be liberated. Freed from externals, you will be detached and independent.

Be self-reliant.

Observe in yourself what is already there.

Farewell.

The zen student is not working for ideas or for understanding in the usual sense. Rinzai's sayings show this. They also show that the understanding for which the student is striving is not mysterious. It is simply an awareness through himself of the world. It begins by just sitting quietly and continues by keeping at this.[1]

14

The hard work: sesshin

THE buildings in a Zen temple compound are, of course, part of a religious institution. An order of monks has its seat there, and at times lay adherents of the sect come for ceremonies and occasional lectures.

These buildings and compounds may, however, be regarded differently. They may be seen as some of the many instruments that facilitate the practice of *zazen*. They make it possible for the beginner in zen study, and they are means by which an advanced student deepens his *zazen*. The compound is, in other words, like a university campus in the West, a place for study.

Some of the large compounds are called mother temples. In each of these, regular "courses" of study are conducted, and Zen monks and lay students come from all over the country for these courses. A normal period of study is three years. Successful completion of Zen studies requires much additional work, but a three-year stint is regarded as adequate for a thorough introduction.

Each of these years is divided into certain periods. For six months, residence in the temple is not required. During this time the student usually returns to his home and pursues his ordinary occupation, though he may remain at the temple and continue his studies. The other six months of the year are divided into two three-month "terms," roughly a winter term and a spring term. During these terms the monks and lay disciples maintain the temple and do *zazen* and *sanzen*, together with the rituals that serve as aids to *zazen*.[1]

Approximately once a month during each of these terms, the zen study is enormously intensified for a week. These weeks are called *sesshin*. ('*Sesshin*' means: to collect thoughts.) During a *sesshin*, work in the temple is cut to a minimum. Every effort is devoted to *zazen* and *sanzen*. The students sit in *zazen* for hours each day and have up to five *sanzen* interviews per day with the *roshi*. The zealous student may go without sleep for the entire *sesshin*, performing *zazen* while the rest indulge in the few hours of sleep a night that are allotted to them by the regulations governing *sesshin*. Except for chanting sutras and *sanzen*, absolute silence is the desideratum. Talking and idle chatter dissipate the concentration for which the student is striving. Movements from one building to another, to meals and so on, are signaled by bells, gongs, and wooden clappers. The atmosphere in the temple becomes so tense that it crackles. The affair would resemble commando training were it not that the results being achieved are so different.

The central building during a *sesshin* is the *zendo* (meditation hall).[2] The student lives here during this period, as well as using it for *zazen*. The days and nights run as follows. At three a.m. the people are awakened by the sound of a gong. They rise instantly, stow their bedding on shelves above the *tan,* and slip out to the washstand. Returning to the *zendo,* they assume a kneeling position on the *tan*. At the sound of a bell they walk in file to the *hondo* (lecture hall). There until a quarter to four they and their *roshi,* who has joined them from his quarters, chant sutras in kneeling or lotus position. Then back to the *zendo,* where they assume the lotus position in *zazen* for an hour. During this time they slip out in turn for *sanzen* with the *roshi*.

A bell sounds at a quarter to five and the people file to the eating hall. Sutras are chanted for five minutes in the lotus position. Breakfast: rice and pickles. At five minutes to five the students return to the *zendo,* where, kneeling, they are served tea by one of their number. A bell. From five to five-thirty there is a break, after which *zazen,* with another *sanzen,* is resumed until seven-thirty.

At seven-thirty working clothes are put on and till ten-thirty weeds in the garden are picked and the buildings swept. At this time the novice may be cautioned that weed-picking is an extension of *zazen.* Occasionally this period is varied. Sometimes there is practice in sutra chanting and a *teisho* (lecture) in the *hondo* from the *roshi.* His custom is to convey the meaning of some Zen Buddhist text. At other times the students beg through the town.[3]

Noon meal is at a quarter to eleven. Rice, pickles, and soup with bean curd. After sutras, silence as usual. The student is concentrating every moment of the day. From eleven to twelve-thirty the people are off, to practice *zazen* on their own, in or out of the *zendo,* and to have another *sanzen.*

From twelve-thirty to two-thirty the *zendo* again. *Zazen.* A third *sanzen.*

From two-thirty to four-thirty more work. At a quarter to five the so-called medicinal meal (Buddhists are not supposed to eat after noon). Rice and pickles. From five to five-thirty, if it is summer, a bath. In winter there is one bath for the week. Five-thirty to six-thirty more "free" *zazen.*

From six-thirty to ten formal *zazen* in the *zendo.* There are five-minute breaks at the half hours for those who need them. As usual a monk walks slowly around the hall bearing a long staff. He can assist those who become stiff or drowsy by judicious blows with this instrument. The students can request this aid, as well as receive it without request, and from time to time the *zendo* resounds with the thwack of wood brought smartly against shoulders and backs.

At seven the *roshi* comes to *zazen* with his students. There is another *sanzen* during the hour from eight to nine. At nine-fifteen the *roshi* reenters the dimly lit *zendo*. Slowly he walks before the *tan,* studying his pupils, straightening those who need it, judging from their posture the depth of their concentration.

At ten a sutra is chanted, tea is served, a bell is rung, and the single light in the hall extinguished. From ten to eleven the people take their cushions out into the garden for more "free" *zazen.* They may return at eleven to sleep if they wish. They may also stay out all night in *zazen* if they will. Sometimes an older monk will pair off with a younger in this, each helping the other to keep awake and at his studies.

A *sesshin* in the winter differs from a *sesshin* in the summer in that the student sleeps, if he will, for only one hour a night instead of four.

Sutra chanting seems strange only because it is an Oriental custom, different from any in the West. So with the rice and pickles. Otherwise there is nothing exotic in a *sesshin.* Nor is there anything incomprehensible. There is only hard work.

That, and something of great importance for *zazen:* no talking and no reading. The student emerges again to reading and talking when he is, so to speak, strong enough to take these quietly. But the way to that is through the quiet of no reading and no talking.

15

Ladder Zen and the paradoxes

SESSHINS do not occur only in Zen temples. Zen students in Japan whose other occupations keep them away from the temples at times of *sesshin* conduct their own *sesshin*, minus *sanzen*, whenever they can at someone's home. The idea is somehow to get in a week of intensive *zazen* every so often. If this has to be accomplished without the help of *sanzen*, it is still one of the important aids to *zazen*. The steps forward that characterize zen study are more likely to occur during a *sesshin* than at other times.

The lay student is apt to get to the halfway mark in *sesshin* and quit. The Zen monk cannot do this because of his vows to the sect. However, he experiences the same phenomenon. He gets to the point where he feels that he cannot go on. The constant *zazen,* often the pain, the orderliness, the silence, being entirely on his own even though he is with others—all take their toll.

However, the monk and the lay student, if he is lucky, then experience something else. Somewhere just past the midpoint of the *sesshin* they find that they can go on. The rest becomes relatively easy. And they finish with a sense of exhilaration that is sometimes profound. This phenomenon resembles that of the "second wind" in athletics. It is also an aspect of the step-like character of zen study, but the likeness it bears to athletics is important. *Zazen* is not meditation in the customary Western sense of that term. It is not an affair of the mind or the soul. It is an affair of the body and the mind.

Thus, something with greater strength than pain or silence is taking its toll during *sesshin*. The reader may already have felt the sort of thing this is. Its occurrence forces real breaking points. In the case of the Western intellectual, for example, it must appear inevitably that zen study smacks of the occult. Such a person must finally come to himself and see that Zen Buddhism is a cult. If this has not occurred to him so far, it will in the matter of the *sesshin*—particularly if he experiences it as distinct from reading about it. Then he hears the gongs, the clacks of the clappers, smells the incense, and sees the bowing to the floor. He sees the long hours of sitting, men facing each other in silence. The monotonous chanting of the sutras is outlandish, and when one is translated for him he is repelled by what he would have to say over and over again if he were to study Zen.[1]

It is all very well, he may think, to speak of egolessness and living in accord with reality, of the spirit of Zen and the Zen person. Blyth says that Don Quixote is the perfect example of the Zen person. But all this other stuff: the ritual, the bells, the incense! The matter is worse than having to work hard; it is primitive and irrational. Sitting quietly for a half an hour a day has the ring of Coué about it, but this other sort of thing takes it beyond the pale. Why should *I* indulge in this?

A theoretical answer is: The question and the feelings that accompany it are similar to those which can cause a zen student to flee a *sesshin*. They are forms of the resistance to *zazen* that the zen student encounters.[2] The resistance extends from *zazen* to all the devices that are aids to zen study: the rituals, the koans, and *sanzen*. The zen student has to cut through these points of resistance. *Zazen* is not simply a matter of sitting quietly, both mentally and physically. It is not simply a matter of keeping thoughts out of one's mind. It cuts deeper; thoughts have roots deeper than imagined.

However, the foregoing is theory. It is of little avail in practice. The zen student must *see* the deeper roots for himself and must cut through the resistances with which he is confronted. As he does, he takes a step forward.

When Bokuju was asked: "We have to dress and eat every day, and how can we escape from all that?" the master replied: "We dress, we eat." "I do not understand you," said the questioner. "If you do not understand, put your dress on and eat your food."

The resistances to *zazen* are subtle and varied. For example, it seems perfectly reasonable to say: "Of course, *you* don't have to take this way. Some need it, others do not." But this line of attack is simply the focus of further resistance. Another step is taken when the student realizes that *you* might or might not take this way, when he realizes that *you* neither have to take it nor to avoid it.

This step may lead to another. The *roshis* are marvelous "devices" for making possible the deepening of *zazen*. Thus they too come into question. Doubts about them arise. Then the student finds that faith is required of him. He finally *sees* that he has to have faith in the practice and faith in his *roshi*. Then he has faith. And because zen study is like an onion, its outer layers resembling its inner, this faith may continue far into the course of zen study—until it turns out to be something quite different, something virtually the opposite of faith: independent strength.

There is, however, the student sees when he first comes across it, nothing irrational about this faith, no matter of releasing himself to the will of another. It is just the sort of thing, except perhaps for its strength, that is exhibited when we ask a stranger for a street direction. He has been where we want to go and we follow his directions. So it is with the zen student and the *roshi*, except that the *roshi* goes along pointing out the route. And evidence that he is on the right track, that the faith is justified, keeps appearing in the experience of the student.

The doubts, as noted, vary. A question is often asked about the lotus position for *zazen*. Why this position rather than any other? The questioner wants an explanation. And he may be given one. He can be told that the position does this and that physiologically for its users, or that it helps the student to turn in on himself. These explanations may be correct. Another step, however, consists in seeing that they are beside the point. The answer to the question is: Those who have used the position report that it works.

There is another way of putting this matter. If you want to study Zen, study it; that is, do *zazen*. If you want explanations (why the lotus position?) you are not interested in Zen; you are interested in explanations. That is all right, but explanations are not Zen and one should be clear about what it is that one is interested in.

However, the doubts reappear. "There is more than one route to a given destination," the student may say to himself. "This is only reasonable. There *are* many routes to the North Pole, and so there must be many ways to the life of the spirit. Why should I take the way of Zen?"

Of course. But where are you now?

From their reading, zen students have learned that the Zen Buddhist is detached, he is egoless, he has no goals. A student may then find himself in the position of thinking that any talk of goals is a mistake. When he tries to tell others what Zen Buddhism or zen study is, he grows impatient with the repeated question: But what is the purpose of all this, what good does it do? It is not a matter of goals and purposes, he replies. You just do it—for its own sake. Or he may say: You cannot talk about the goals of zen study for there are no goals in Zen.

Then it finally occurs to him. Why, he asks himself, have I been so concerned not to talk about goals? Why has the word 'goals' been such a bugbear? There is nothing wrong with talking of goals if you are not attached to nor *compulsively detached* from 'goals.'

After that he is able to say: The goal of zen study is tranquillity. He may think of the Zen story of two monks who were traveling. They came to a stream where they found a pretty young woman who could not cross without soiling her dress. The older of the two monks picked her up and carried her across. The younger followed, horrified by this trifling with their vows of celibacy. The monks went on their way. After some time the younger monk could stand it no longer. He burst out: "We monks don't go near women. How could you have done that?" The older monk looked at him and said: "Are you still carrying that girl around? I put her down miles back."

Zen is not a matter of goals. The goal of Zen study is tranquillity. The so-called paradoxes of Zen Buddhism are resolved by taking such steps as those discussed in this chapter. With each step the student sees logic in something in which he saw only contradiction before. That may be why parables and stories convey more, in talk about Zen Buddhism, than logical discourse does. As the student takes step after step he appreciates the fact that there is nothing illogical in Zen. It is the student who is illogical, and he is so only because he cannot see the logic of the matter. On the other hand, he comes to see its logic not by ratiocination but by living through the paradoxical, by taking steps on his own.

Consider a question that is asked by wives of men who have undertaken zen study. These wives do some reading and shortly get the idea. The question is: If you pursue this study and are successful with it, what becomes of our relation? You will become selfless and detached. What will happen to *me?*

If this question is taken seriously, how can it be answered? It cannot be, although it has an answer. The beginner in zen study may fall into the trap of trying to reason it out. He will come across fine theories. The detached man is *really* the attached man, for example. But none of these do. Finally he may see that the question is his wife's "koan." It is a sign of something in *her,* some point of resistance to change. Thus, *he* can never answer the question. She will have to answer it herself by taking a step on her own, by seeing, perhaps, that her "love" for her husband is not love but a need. Then she may see that she does not need him. Then she will find him still around. For that is the way they live.

An important step occurs when the student sees that *zazen itself is a device.* For then he is on the way to seeing that just doing it is what he is striving for, whether he feels that he is accomplishing anything or not. It becomes clear that he can get as wrapped up in the idea of *zazen* as he can get wrapped up in any idea. He can come to think that it is leading to something far more significant than *it* is. The grass is always greener on the other side. However, the goal is the practice. The student has seen more deeply into another of the "paradoxes" and it makes more sense.

16

Some history

ACCORDING to Heinrich Dumoulin, a historian of Zen Buddhism, the first Western contact with Zen came in the sixteenth century, when Christian missionaries visited Japan. There they encountered the doctrine of nothingness, had conversations with *roshis,* were impressed with the tea ceremony, and, according to their reports, made conversions even among the *roshis.* They probably did not know that a Zen Buddhist would agree to conversion simply to facilitate relations with the foreigners. On the other hand, they may have found out, for they came to regard the Zen sect as the most satanic of the Buddhist sects.

Since then there has not been much contact between the West and Zen Buddhism. Certainly there has not been contact with Zen Buddhism in Japan until recently, for the doors of Japan were closed to the West for two hundred and fifty years before 1854. When the West did become interested in Buddhism, about one hundred and fifty years ago, it was not Zen Buddhism with which it became acquainted. Rather it was the Buddhism in India. A knowledge of Sino-Japanese Buddhism is in fact quite recent, and its accuracy has been impaired by the prior and longer knowledge of Indian Buddhism, which is a horse of another though not entirely different color.

The story of the recent coming of Zen Buddhism to the West is largely that of the coming of Japanese Zen Buddhism.[1] Some awareness of it is important, for the story, even when briefly told, makes it clear that the coming of Zen to the West is in the main a literary phenomenon in which *zazen* has been neglected.

Although there are now a number of Westerners engaged in zen study in Japan, the transmission of Zen to the West has so far been the work of surprisingly few individuals. Apart from the very few Westerners, such as Eugen Herrigel,[2] who were zen students in Japan and then wrote of the study, or the somewhat larger number of people who heard of Zen in the West and began writing about it, Zen was brought to the West by a small band of Japanese Zen Buddhists who trace their teaching to Engaku Temple in Kamakura. Of these only one is well known, D. T. Suzuki.

After the 1850's, when Japan was opened to the West, the *roshi* at Engaku-ji was Kosen. He became a famous teacher during the Meiji Era, in part because he took an equally keen interest in the promulgation of Zen among laymen and in the lay education of Zen Buddhist monks. He was aware, too, that Zen Buddhism was in danger of dying out in the rapidly modernizing Japan of his day, and he cherished the idea of its transmission to the West, where it might flourish again. For some reason Kosen was under the impression that, of all the Western countries, the United States would provide the best soil for the Zen seeds that would be carried from Japan.

This interest in the transmission of Zen to the West was not a missionary interest. The Zen Buddhist does not go forth to help others with his teaching. He waits for them to come to him, when he will give of it freely. For he is a Zen, that is, a meditating Buddhist, and he knows that the pupil must want the teaching before it can be used. The interest in transmitting Zen to the West may best be likened, I think, to the interest of the painter in his art. He would little love to see this thing of infinite value die out. When it was threatened in one place he might carry it to another, not to bring painting to others but to preserve painting.

However that may be, Kosen's activities included meditation weeks held for distinguished laymen in Tokyo and the eventual formation of this group into a society. The lay group was formed with the idea that it would be used in the transmission of Zen to the West. Kosen also required Soyen Shaku, his most brilliant disciple, to attend one of the first Japanese universities devoted to the study of Western culture.

In his turn Soyen Shaku became a great *roshi*. Among his disciples in the 1880's were two young lay students, D. T. Suzuki and Sekibutsu Koji, the latter of whom later took Shaku's name and came to be called Sokatsu Shaku. In 1893 Soyen Shaku was invited to the World Parliament of Religions in Chicago. He went, taking with him D. T. Suzuki as translator and becoming the first Zen priest to visit the West. When he returned to Japan, Suzuki stayed behind to work as a translator. Eventually Sokatsu finished his Zen studies with Soyen and, after some travel, was ordained and commissioned by Soyen to go to Tokyo and continue Kosen's work with lay students, which had fallen in abeyance after Kosen's death in 1892.

In 1905 Soyen Shaku again went to the United States as a result of a visit from Mr. and Mrs. Alexander Russell at Engaku-ji. He gave a number of lectures, which were translated, edited, and published by Suzuki. This is the book called *Sermons of a Buddhist Abbot*.

Meanwhile Sokatsu Shaku had established a small temple in

the suburbs of Tokyo. Many of his students were drawn from the Imperial University of Tokyo. In 1906 he took six of his disciples to San Francisco with the intention of establishing a Zen temple in that city. The group included a graduate in philosophy from the University of Tokyo, Zuigan Goto, and a young art student, Shigetsu Sasaki. After four years of futile struggle, Sokatsu Shaku decided that the West was not yet ready for Zen and returned to his homeland with five of his students. One, Shigetsu Sasaki, remained in the United States.

After nine years of wandering across the country, Shigetsu found himself in New York in 1919. During these years he had continued his *zazen*, and in that year he decided to return to his *roshi* to complete his Zen study. Finally in 1928 he returned to New York as Sokei-an Roshi, charged by his teacher to bring Zen to the Occident. Sokatsu had thought that he would be better received as a layman; but Shigetsu differed with him, believing that the dignity of his church would assist his work. Thus, Shigetsu Sasaki became the first Zen *roshi* to make his home in the West.

Meanwhile, early in the 1900's, a wandering Zen monk had come to California. This was Nyogen Senzaki, who lived for fifty years, mainly in Los Angeles, quietly teaching Zen Buddhism. Elsewhere, Suzuki had commenced and carried on his prodigious writing career. By 1928 with the publication of his *Essays in Zen Buddhism* (*First Series*) he began to be fairly widely read. Various Buddhist societies in Europe and the United States, which had been oriented to Indian Buddhism and were often outgrowths of Theosophical Societies, began to be interested in Zen Buddhism. Largely because of the writings of this one man, and later to the writings of those who were interested by his work, the absorption with Zen in the West was on its way. It was an interest that mounted so rapidly after World War II that there has been talk of the Zen Boom in the United States.

In spite of the growing interest in Zen in the thirties few people came to listen to and to sit with Sokei-an Roshi. But he worked quietly and doggedly on at the Hermitage of Sokei, which he established in New York City in 1930 as the first Zen temple in the West. In late December of 1941 his work perforce came to an end, and Sokei-an found himself in a detention camp for enemy aliens. Released in 1944 because of ill-health and the efforts of his disciples, he married one of them, an American, Ruth Fuller Everett. In May, 1945, he died at the age of sixty-three.

As the story goes, Sokei-an charged Mrs. Sasaki with three tasks before his death. One was to return to Japan, where she had engaged in Zen studies in the 1930's, and find a *roshi* who would come to the United States and continue Sokei-an's work. Another was to make possible translations of Zen texts that are needed for Zen teaching. The third task was the establishment of a center for Zen study for Westerners in Japan.

Mrs. Sasaki has since been hard at work at the successful accomplishment of these charges. She has made possible the installation of Isshu Miura Roshi as the permanent *roshi* of The First Zen Institute of New York. She has assembled a team of translators in Kyoto to provide translations of important Zen texts. And in 1958 she was ordained a priestess in the Rinzai Sect of Zen Buddhism at Daitoku-ji in Kyoto, where the center for Zen study for Westerners has since been established. It is called The First Zen Institute of America in Japan. Its central building is the *zendo*.

Finally, in the story of the coming of Zen to the Occident, there was the interest that Nyogen Senzaki showed in the poetry of a *roshi* in Japan, Soen Nakagawa. As a result of a correspondence that developed between them, Soen Nakagawa paid his first visit to the United States early in the 1950's, when he came to call on Senzaki in Los Angeles. Later, in 1958, he returned to Los Angeles after Senzaki's death and visited with the latter's small following. In 1960, Soen Nakagawa came again. By now he had not only these people in Los Angeles to help with their zen study; he had American students in his own temple in Japan. He held a *sesshin* during this visit. There were some twenty people who attended it irregularly and four or five who were there for the whole time.

What is the bearing of this story, sketchy as it is, on the practice of Zen? The story shows that direct contact with Zen in the West has been extremely limited. A handful of Zen Buddhists have visited the West. On the other hand, hundreds of books and articles have been written about Zen. The coming of Zen to the West has been so far almost entirely a literary phenomenon. *Zazen* does not feature in it.

When asked about the Zen Boom in the United States, Goto Roshi said: "It's a firecracker," and laughed until the tears streamed down his cheeks.

17

The theory

THE theory behind Zen Buddhism is simple. It can be and has been endlessly complicated—possibly a form of resistance to its practice. The fact remains, however, that the theory is simple. It is, moreover, extremely empirical. That is to say, it can be verified in the experience of anyone. Zen Buddhism is a radical empiricism.

The theory has two parts: the Buddhist and the Zen. According to Siddhartha, the Buddha, men's lives are predominantly unhappy. There is in each life, of course, some happiness. But by and large unhappiness is the lot of men. This results from the facts that everything changes and that men refuse to accept the change in selfish craving for stability. An example of the ceaseless change is death. In this case the refusal to accept change often takes form in the idea of personal immortality, i.e., the belief that one does not *really* die.

However, the selfish craving for permanence, the opposition to change, can be controlled. The lives of some, notably the life of the Buddha himself, testify to this. The result is happiness. All that is required, then, is a method for establishing the control.

In point of historical fact the method used by the Buddha was meditation. He tried others, but this worked for him. Historical account also has it that the Buddha himself used various teachings in his efforts to help others with their struggle for control. For example, during one period of his life he taught the use of the eightfold path. At another time, when asked to instruct a large group, he simply held up a flower and gazed at it in silence. It is reported that one of the audience, Mahakasyapa, a favorite disciple, smiled. Whereupon the Buddha said that Mahakasyapa alone understood the teaching.

A different way of putting the second portion of the theory is the Zen way. Selfish craving can be controlled. The key to control is enlightenment. The means for obtaining enlightenment is *zazen*, together with the various aids to *zazen* which have been found useful. The evidence that this method works lies in the lives of its users.

Thus the theory is simple. It is confirmed in everyday private experience; though the matter may be otherwise in public where one hesitates to admit to his private experiences. The only hard thing about the theory is the practice. The doing is difficult, so endless theories are constructed about it and about the particular theory that lies behind it. The simple hard core is thereby lost sight of. A mystery is made of a matter, the matter, which is mysterious only in its simplicity.

What of the Zen stories, then, and the tremendous number of Buddhist texts and sutras? The stories with their paradoxes and their non sequiturs surely indicate something out of this world. The sutras and texts are usually of great difficulty and have an esoteric ring. They seem to speak of something more than this simple theory implies.

An answer is: The stories are often koans and are to be used like koans in helping a student with his *zazen*. For one not performing *zazen*, one who has not arrived at the impasse that the story might break, the stories become mere intellectual puzzles and very odd ones. The sutras and texts, too, are teaching aids, which only appear extraordinary when read out of the context of the practice.

It may be added that both the stories and the texts can often function as teaching aids because they are descriptions of how a person feels when he makes a step in the practice. It is easy, on the other hand, for one trained in Western thought to take the texts, particularly, as though they were theories about reality and to overlook their instrumental value or their value as expressions of great achievement.[1]

Finally, of course, the stories and sutras come out of a culture different from our own. The language, even when it is English, is strange. Perhaps, if the practice were to spread to the West, a fresh growth of sutras and stories would occur—one with more familiar scent.

18

Zen and psychoanalysis

INTEREST in the possible relations between Zen and psychoanalysis is growing. It may be justified. It seems unlikely, however, that sound exploration of these possible relations will occur until it is undertaken by individuals thoroughly experienced in each of the practices.

The subject is raised here only because it can direct further attention to *zazen*. For example, most of what has been said and written about the possible connections between Zen and psychoanalysis has been said or written by people who have experienced either one or the other but not both. Unhappily some of it has been said by persons who have experienced neither. Thus, most if not all the talk stems from theory and speculation and not from experience. It is, therefore, another way in which the practice of Zen is obscured. And this in the face of the fact that only practice gives the kind of "knowledge" in which the Zen Buddhist is interested: direct experience.

It is also useful to point out that, although there is some evidence that sitting quietly may help in analytic therapy, there is no evidence that analytic techniques would have any bearing in *zazen*. The reason for this is simple. There are no *roshis* who are psychoanalysts.[1] Furthermore, when something *like zazen* is used in therapy, its use is different from the use of *zazen* in zen study. Remember that the practice and its goal are identical in *zazen*.

Nevertheless, people want to say, the Zen Buddhist is the calm, detached person and in therapy the patient is seeking a kind of detachment, some sort of freedom. There are, therefore, resemblances between analysis and Zen.

True. However, there are also resemblances between tennis and Zen. Both require practice and discipline; in both there are physical exercise and moments of exultation. In other words, resemblances *and* differences may be noted anywhere; but only experience will show whether the awareness of them is instructive or otherwise.

To go further, taking into account the proposition that no one is completely "normal" and that, therefore, everyone could use analysis, the possibility of relations between Zen and psycho-analysis may be thought of as follows. The practice of *zazen* is for the well, and analytic therapy for the ill. The word 'therapy' suggests this important difference. There is also the evidence that individuals with severe psychological disturb-ances cannot stand the strain of *zazen* and *sanzen*. Some direct acquaintance with *zazen* further confirms that there is this dif-ference between Zen and psychoanalysis.

An analogy with something physical makes the difference clearer. A person does not think of having an exploratory operation unless there are signs that something is wrong. These operations, like other medical devices, are for the sick, not the well. Now consider psychoanalysis. It is a going into the psyche to discover something that is causing trouble. Under normal conditions one would not be inclined, then, to urge a psychoanalysis (unless, as is the practice, it were for training purposes).

The analogy not only suggests that Zen and psychoanalysis are fundamentally different. It also leads to seeing something about *zazen*. Although it is a way of knowing oneself, *zazen* is not "psycho" analysis in the way that psychoanalysis is. The latter is ego analysis, an actual exploration of the ego. In *zazen* the student certainly comes up against the ego, in more senses of that term than the one in which the psychoanalyst employs it. However, he is trying to know the ego in the manner in which he comes to know the rest of himself in *zazen,* that is, directly. The object of this knowing is not analysis of the ego in any sense of that term.[2] The student is learning to control it, in part, by this direct awareness, for the rest, by the strength that is coming from his discipline. There is, then, a kind of objectivity as distinct from subjectivity in the task he is performing. This is sometimes noted by saying that Zen practice is impersonal. It is neither masculine nor feminine. It is neuter.

This character of neutrality is observable in Zen gardens, which are famous for their simplicity, for the absence of lushness in them, for their rigor, their strength, and their severity—all of which are marks of the practicing Zen Buddhist. There is, to put it otherwise, an unemotional quality about Zen practice. *Zazen* not only symbolizes these qualities: it is these qualities.

To return to the possible relations between Zen and psychoanalysis: the foregoing picture is far removed from that of the emotionally disturbed person who is valiantly battling his way out of an affliction with the trained and sympathetic aid of the analyst.

19

Zen and philosophy

OFTEN, when the fact that the basis of Zen lies in *zazen* is made clear, people ask whether the quiet sitting cannot be performed in a chair. The answer is, of course, that it can be. The question may then be pursued, particularly when it has also become clear that *zazen* comes to pervade a person's whole life, Cannot *zazen* be practiced on a walk in the mountains? Again the answer must be, yes. Even during a game of golf? Yes, even in golf. At this point sighs of relief rise. "Why I have been doing *zazen* for years." It is a relief to find that the matter can apparently be made familiar and that nothing needs to be changed by it.

That relief may be seen as a sign of the resistance to *zazen* that the zen student experiences in so many forms. The reader may have experienced a similar sort of relief during the last two chapters, where the ground was familiar again: theories and arguments. The fact is, however, as *zazen* shows, that a great deal has to be changed.

There is a story that indicates clearly the variety and subtlety of the gambits that can appear in this matter. "The pupils of the Tendai school used to study meditation before Zen entered Japan. Four of them who were intimate friends promised one another to observe seven days of silence.

"On the first day all were silent. Their meditation had begun auspiciously, but when night came and the oil lamps were growing dim one of the pupils could not help exclaiming to a servant: 'Fix those lamps.'

"The second pupil was surprised to hear the first one talk. 'We are not supposed to say a word,' he remarked.

"'You two are stupid. Why did you talk?' asked the third.

"'I am the only one who has not talked,' concluded the fourth pupil."[1]

It is more deeply significant that we feel relief when confronted with theory in the midst of fact and that we play these games. The relief and the games are signs of resistance to such aspects of zen practice as the hard work and the ceaseless vigilance. They are also marks of one of men's essential characteristics. We are mental as well as physical creatures. And this must be taken into account in the practice of Zen. In part, it is thus that the koan exercise is used as an adjunct to *zazen*. Furthermore, the Zen Buddhist insists that the state of no-mind is not a condition of mere vacuity.

The matter may be regarded in another way. The resistance to the practice is mental as well as physical. This may be noticed in the questions that are asked about *zazen* in the effort to make it easy or to write it off. The same sort of thing appears in the disparaging views that can be expressed when the issue of ritual is raised. The mind is cunning.

The mind is also profound, and the mental aspect of resistance goes far deeper than these questions, views, and little tricks indicate. These depths are revealed in the form of colossal doubt, which finds expression in a strikingly curious sort of question.

These questions are curious because they appear so insuperably difficult to answer as to be even nonsensical, whereas their answers, once obtained, are seen to be simple and straightforward. In Zen Buddhism certain of these questions are koans. In the West, where there is also that resistance to change with which the Buddhist struggles, these questions have been called philosophical or metaphysical.

Here are some examples of these questions, first in their Eastern forms. What is the cardinal principle of Buddhism? Why did Bodhidharma come from the West (to China)? Does the dog have Buddha-nature or not? Western forms:

Does God exist? Is there immortality? What is the meaning of life?

The Buddhist has been told that the Buddha said that all sentient beings (and, therefore, the dog) have Buddha-nature. Still he asks: Does the dog have Buddha-nature? The Westerner has been assured that life has meaning. Nevertheless, he can ask with gnawing doubt: But does it *really?*

There is a tradition in Western thought according to which these fundamental questions are unanswerable. It is the skeptic tradition. In its most recent form, the philosophy called logical positivism, it has become the view that these questions cannot be answered because they are meaningless questions. They look sensible because of their grammatical form, but when examined carefully they turn out to be no better than the question: Was it brillig and did the slithy toves gyre and gimble in the wabe?

Some positivists have gone on to develop the view that these "fundamental" questions occur as a result of misuses of language and that they disappear when we get straightened out about language. Others have said that they are puzzlements that require a kind of therapy. In any case, they are not to be dealt with as though they were serious. They are like the question of a child at night about goblins. You do not look for the goblin in the child's room, as though his question were a real one. Instead you seek the cause for his crying out and asking about goblins. Was he wakened and frightened because of what he ate? So with philosophic questions. One does not try to answer them. Instead one asks what made a person ask them. The outcome of the "therapy" is that ultimately the questions disappear or dissolve.

The Buddhist has reacted a little like the skeptic to these questions. In the koan exercise, however, the Zen Buddhist uses them as a means for controlling the resistance to the practice. Instead of trying to find a way around the questions, the student is made to go through them until he finds the simple answer at the other end of the resistance that has kept him from seeing it before. The koan is used like a sword for cutting down through the resistance to the point where the student masters it instead of it him.

In curious ways, to carry the matter further, the Zen Buddhist is getting at the same thing as the positivist, though there is an important difference between them. Regarded from one level, the questions *are* meaningless. However, the Zen *roshi* endeavors to get the student to see the meaninglessness itself. This is the emptiness, void, egolessness, the nothing of which the Zen Buddhist talks.[2] And in the course of this koan exercise, which is work with a koan and not analysis of a koan, the student's intellect is respected and even turned to the task of aiding the practice. The questions are taken seriously, but they are *used* for a specific purpose. Again one sees that it is the practice that counts, all else, intellectual and otherwise, being employed instrumentally for this.

As the student probes to deeper levels he finds that the questions have answers after all. Only something in him has prevented him from seeing them. The outcome is the acceptance of the change that he has been resisting. The questions are then left behind, and one thinks again of the positivist's view that the questions are not really important.

What are the simple answers to these deep questions? Does the dog have Buddha-nature or not? *Mu* (no). What is the cardinal principle of Buddhism? There is a cypress in the courtyard. Why did Bodhidharma come from the West? That is the same question as the one about the cardinal principle. Does life have meaning? Yes—the meaning you give it. Is there immortality? Yes, being free is being immortal. The business about life after death is a metaphorical way of putting this. When it is taken literally it is a way of resisting change. Does God exist? Only in the minds of men.[3]

"Before you have studied Zen, mountains are mountains and rivers are rivers; while you are studying it, mountains are no longer mountains and rivers no longer rivers; but once you have had Enlightenment, mountains are once again mountains and rivers are rivers."[4]

20

Ryoan-ji: the practice again

ZAZEN too, then, is an instrument. It is, however, an instrument of a special kind, for it is identical with
that which it fashions. It fashions *zazen*. Pictures of this can
be given verbally, but the best pictures of it are non-verbal
such as the triangle and the toy of *Daruma*. When *zazen is*
pictured verbally, its finest likenesses appear in anecdotes or
images like "the calm ocean within."
The preceding four chapters show this. There attention was
being directed to *zazen* and aspects of it being brought out
by means of theories and abstractions. The danger in this is

evident when it is pointed out, for abstractions lead ever away from the concrete.

The clearest picture of the goal of *zazen* is *zazen*. Here the goal is seen fully and directly: calm, stability, strength, simplicity, intensity, rigor.

When a zen student is presented with a koan by his *roshi,* he already has the "problem" in the koan in the depths of his mind. The question, What is the cardinal principle of Buddhism? equals the question, Why did Bodhidharma come from the West? equals the question, What is Zen? Although the reader may have picked up this book in idle curiosity or with a desire to be informed, the chances are that something different was at work. What *is* Zen? The question is a koan. The answer to it can come only through *zazen*. The answer is *zazen;* but this can only be known by *zazen,* by "knowing" *zazen,* by doing it.

When the monk asked Joshu whether the dog has Buddha-nature or not, Joshu replied: *"Mu!"* 'Mu' means 'no,' and 'nothing' and 'emptiness.' At some point in their training of the zen student, different *roshis* use different methods. Some have the students sit during *zazen* facing the wall and shouting *"Mu"* over and over again by the hour. Others have the students hiss *"Mu."* Another will have his students sit quietly, each imagining *mu* being draped over him from head to foot. Drastic measures are needed to bring about fully the answer to a question like "What is Zen?" when it is a koan or puzzlement. (Otherwise the answer is simple: Meditation Buddhism.)

On the other hand, the start must be made somewhere. A glimpse of Zen may do this. In the frontispiece of the book is a picture of the rock garden at the Zen temple, Ryoan-ji. The garden embodies the rigor, the simplicity, the tranquillity, the intensity, and the strength that come with *zazen*. Hard and constant work is required to preserve this garden as it is. There must be daily care.

The rocks jutting up from the calm surface are like the thoughts that rear to distract the quiet of the zen student. They are also related to another Zen story. One day Sen no Rikyu asked a disciple to rake their garden. The monk worked assiduously and at length. This was to be a perfect job for the master. Finally, when the monk was through, Rikyu came to inspect. He took one look and then shook a tree so that a few leaves fell. "That's better," he said. . . . The perfectly clean garden represents an attachment to an ideal, another idea of which the disciple had to be rid. The garden at Ryoan-ji would be imperfect without the rocks.

It has been said that men have no language for the life of the spirit, for the inner as contrasted with the outer life. We have only the language that refers to the objective world, the world of things. If we are to speak of the inner, we must borrow from the language of the outer and can, thus, only be misleading and misled.

The garden at Ryoan-ji goes a step beyond this view, for the garden tells the story of the inner life. And it shows that the language of the outer *is* the language of the inner when it has the characteristics of this garden: when it is untroubled.

21

Listening

AS the zen student struggles with himself or with his koan, which comes to the same thing, he may be advised to watch the *roshi*. "Look at the old man," a student who is further along with the matter may say. "Look at the old man carefully; watch everything that he does when you go in for *sanzen*." Then the student may see that the *roshi* is showing him the answer he seeks. It is even simpler than that. The old man sitting there quietly *is* the answer for one of the koans. He shows the answer by being it.

However, watching the *roshi* carefully is difficult for the student. It may be months or years before he is able to do this.

For there is in the student an almost insurmountable tendency to *interpret* what the *roshi* says or does instead of taking it just as it is. The student strives to find the *meaning* of that imperturbable figure before him, or the *meaning* of that quick gesture or utterance. He cannot believe that it is as simple as it is, that the *roshi* sitting there quietly is the answer to this koan.

There is in this another way of describing *zazen*. It is learning to listen. It is learning to accept. "Listen to the old man." Do not interpret. So it is with the triangle. Look at *it*. It is the lesson it is teaching. So it is, too, with talking. Talking about Zen is all right if it is pointing to Zen. But the pointer must not be mistaken for the thing pointed to. One has to learn to listen. The zen student does this by practicing *zazen* and more *zazen*.

Once in Japan, shortly before commencing zen study and while he was still reading everything concerning it on which hand could be laid, a foreigner was invited by a Japanese acquaintance to visit his teacher, a Zen Buddhist. The foreigner was delighted with the prospect until he learned that the teacher did not speak English. The Japanese smiled when he saw the signs of disappointment appear. "You can learn a great deal about Zen by just meeting a man who is advanced in Zen studies," he said. "Simply observing his manner will teach you much." The foreigner, however, declined the invitation.

He wanted to talk when he met a master. He had so many questions.

One day "Gensha [a master] mounted the platform and after a moment of silence gave this out: 'Do you know it? Do you now recognize it?' So saying he went back to his room. Another time after a silence he simply said, 'This is your true man, just this.'

"One day Gensha remained too long in silence, and the monks thinking he was not going to say anything began to disperse, when the master called them back and denounced them in the following way: 'As I see, you are all cut out of the same pattern, there is none among you who is endowed with any amount of wisdom. When I part my lips you all gather about me wanting to catch my words and speculate on them. But when I really try to do you good, you do not at all know me. If you go on like this, be sure that great trouble is indeed ahead of you.'

"On another occasion he was a little better, for he gave this after a period of silence: 'I am doing what I can for your edification, but do you understand?' " [1]

Interpretation is meant to clarify a passage in a book, but interpretation can be mistaken for the passage. Ideas may help in living, but they can also get in the way.

One sunny morning in Japan after being confined to the house by rain, I walked by a friend's house to go with him to a ceremony. When I arrived I remarked about the weather and said that I would wait for him in the sunny street. "No," he said, "Come and enjoy the garden." And he arranged cushions so that I could view the garden from the house.

When he left to dress, I stepped out onto a rock and became immersed in the garden.

Later after the ceremony cushions were again spread for us to sit and admire the garden. I said, "I'll go out on that rock and get some sun. We can still talk." "Oh, you shouldn't do that," he replied. "The garden is designed to be viewed from this room. You can't see it properly by being in it." I was impressed with this notion. But when I gazed at the garden, trying to see its beauty—I failed.

The story of the fan helps here. A teacher handed one disciple a fan and asked him what it was. The disciple handed it back and said: "A fan." The teacher frowned and handed it to another pupil. This man said not a word. Instead he scratched his back with the fan, poked the *hibachi* with it, opened it, fanned himself; then, placing a gift on it, he handed it to the teacher. The teacher smiled.

As with the idea of the fan, so with the idea of the garden. It got in the way. The garden could no longer be listened to.

Definition of a mystic: a man who can have more than himself in his life, that is, a man who can listen. A mystic is a man who can accept.

22

Lectures I[1]

RELIGION is garbed by the time, the place, and the nature of the people who have it. For example, Christ was persecuted and this shows up in the religion of Christianity. In Mohammedism stealing is not the crime that it is in Christianity because there was a scarcity of food in early Mohammedan countries. This is an example of environmental influences on religion.

I would like you to be clear about this point first. Get it into your head and keep it there.

Next point. The times before the Buddha resembled those

before Luther. The Brahmins were in power and were un-scrupulous.

The fundamental teaching of Buddhism is emancipation. The question is: How to get it? (Christians have become enslaved by the idea of God.) The Buddha studied with all the Brahmin sages and hermits to find out. He failed. So he wiped out the past and started *zazen*. This he practiced from the age of twenty-five to thirty-one according to historians, from the age of twenty to thirty-one according to religious authorities. At any rate, it was for a long time. He washed away the past, all other methods. He literally bathed in a river and ac-cepted milk from a maid, whereupon his retainers left him. He gave up all other methods, such as sitting on nails and what not.

Zazen has some connections with Yoga techniques, but other-wise Buddhism has not. The Buddha sat under the tree for six years. He sat in the triangle (lotus) position, abandoning others. Recent excavations show that the *zazen* position is very ancient and that it predates Yoga practices. However, you can check the historical data for yourself. I am not interested in the question whether *zazen* is a Yoga practice. The important point is that the Buddha did *zazen*.

Now what is the aim of sitting? Emancipation. From what? From the desires for: excessive honor, money, power, sexual pleasure, and sleep. Looked at differently, one sits to emanci-pate oneself from life, old age, sickness, and death;[2] from seeking impossible things; from the fear of being separated from those whom you love. In short, the goal is to get rid of pain and suffering.

Man is in slavery. The idea is to get free. One can imagine man as being trapped in a box. Some try to get free by breaking the box. The Mahayana Buddhist method is to get free without breaking the box. This is done by looking into oneself. What is the *I?* And finding that we have to transcend the opposites, for example, that of the masculine and the feminine. Transcending the opposites is what the Buddha did for six years. Then his eyes were opened and this brought emancipation, *Nirvana,* which is quiet and calmness. To have the bonds on you makes no difference if you are calm.

A new point. 'Zen' comes from '*dhyana,*' which means thinking calmly or calm thinking or carefully weighed thinking. The things that disturb us are not outside but within. The Buddha learned this by self-reflection.

The goal is emancipation from bondage. By Zen or Zen-like training. All the Buddha's teaching came from *zazen,* so Zen training is *zazen.*

All religions must have a basic *zazen*-like training. Why? Because you have to have a firm starting point. Before you start to move forward you have to have a good start. And the busier a person is, the more important *zazen* is.

Zuigan Osho, a great master, asked himself every day: "Master?" He replied: "Yes, Sir." "Be aware." "Yes, Sir." "In the future do not be deceived by men." "Yes, Sir." This was his whole teaching and training: he asked and answered himself thus.

For me Zen means only: quiet, calm, meditation.

I did not go to the United States when I was asked to because one has to teach Zen here in Japan where one will not tell people what they want to hear and where they will see it as it is.

The Americans are a mixture and, therefore, they are frank. But they have no base. Therefore, Zen would be good for them.

Americans need the spiritual union of mind and body to get a basis for their culture. Zen might furnish it.

The East has developed spiritually because it is poor materially.

Zen has been misinterpreted to the West because the interpreters have not finished their training. So they have talked of goals instead of the method.

Americans can transform Zen after they have learned it in Japan. But the learning must come first in Japan.

(Remember that religion varies with the time, the place, and the people who clothe it.)

You cannot take art treasures out of their environment. They have to be seen there. Later, having seen them, you can do what you will with them in your own art.

The Japanese cannot modify Zen for Americans, as the interpreters have tried to do. Americans have to learn it first and then modify it for themselves.

A tribe modifies religion for itself, but first it has to get religion.

The interpreters are egoists, not Buddhists. Furthermore, a man must have a feeling for humanity in order to be able to transmit a teaching. He must be like Goethe or Beethoven.

The more sincere you are, the fewer the people who will listen to you. You get on a higher level and fewer can follow. If a lot of people listen to you, you are no good.

When Zuigan called to himself, "master," he was referring to the man in the box. And the 'do not be deceived by men' meant 'do not be deceived by money, fame, etc.'

Next point: the first sermon of the Buddha. After six years of *zazen,* he taught the eightfold path for getting his enlightenment, to help ordinary people to it. (1) Correct seeing (seeing things just as they are). (2) Right thinking. (This presupposes right seeing, for you need right ideas for right thinking. Right thinking is thinking of things as they are. We can miss doing this by, for example, under or overestimating ourselves. So right thinking also requires a knowledge of yourself.) (3) Right speaking (expressing what you have thought correctly). (4) Right action. (5) Right effort. (Each step is based on the previous ones.) (6) Right determination (that which does not waver after the action is started). (7) Right faith. (8) Right living.

Only these eight steps are necessary for emancipation. There is no need to bow to anyone, etc.

You should experience with your body and not with your head.

Why is there *sanzen,* you ask? By going through contradictions you come to the understanding which goes with *mu* or being nothing.[3] Also, you get to the point where you think that you understand. One who is further along finds that you do not. He discovers this in *sanzen* and can help you. Furthermore, a koan is a way of helping you to cut out your ego. Finally, it is impossible for you now to understand the use of the koan in this practice. You have to accept its use on faith. Later would you come to understand its role.

A genius can accomplish emancipation by sitting alone. In Rinzai Zen we do it step by step. So it is often called ladder Zen.

23

Lectures II

I WANT to continue my exposition and talk of the Kegon philosophy, the philosophy of Zen Buddhism. But first some preliminary remarks and a clarification of the previous lecture.

I observed, during my early experiences with my own teacher, that young girls of, say twenty, went ahead more rapidly with their koans than men did. My teacher explained that this was due to the fact that they had had less experience than the men. However, he said that men, who have to go through more to get there than the girls do, get a firmer base in the end. And I noticed that the girls later slipped more easily.

I want to call your attention to the fact that there is no "method" in Zen study. It is solely a matter of your becoming something. At the university you were taught how to study and helped along in a positive way. In Zen study you are put on your own and the teacher leads you only by preventing you from going astray.

Descartes drew a wrong conclusion from the *cogito:* namely, thinking is accurate. Kant saw that thinking may err. And so in Zen study the teacher is on guard to keep the student from going astray in his thinking. The teaching is really leading you out. Indian Yogis and teachers tell you *what* you have to become.

Finally, the Zen Sect is the most vital in Buddhism because its adherents stress meditation.

Now I shall examine what I said the other day from another angle or, indeed, from the reverse side. In the Sermon on the Mount Christ said: "Blessed are the poor in spirit." This is what the Zen Buddhist is getting at with the teaching of no-mind. And note that Christian texts can furnish examples for Zen Buddhists. Whereas other religions say of each other that the teachings of the other are false, the Zen Buddhist can find the truth in the teachings of any religion.

Zen Buddhist philosophers have always practiced *zazen.* But they have also employed a certain teaching: (1) The way (*tao*) of the adult is to make clear his own (clear) virtue (in Zen Buddhism the latter is called his Buddha-nature). (2) Following this, he should help others to achieve the same condition. (3) Then in the long run all people should live peacefully. This is what the Buddhists call *Nirvana*.

Now, how do we achieve these three things? By five steps: (a) stopping all disturbances in you from the environment; (b) *samadhi* (getting fixed into motionlessness); (c) being quiet; (d) being at ease; and (e) examining yourself (What is this I?).

(Note that these five elements in the Kegon "how" are not so much ways of achieving peace as they are steps in the process.)

What is it that you attain by this? Quiet. You proceed by going over and over these five steps, each time getting a bit better at it. You get calm one day and then you see that this was not calm and you make another step. You have to keep on and on and on. By training you can bring yourself to keep on developing.

The foregoing is a clarification of the previous lecture. Now for the Kegon philosophy (contained in the Kegon Sutra).

Out of the mud can come a lotus.

Consider the Crystal Palace of Indra. In each crystal every other crystal is reflected. And that reflection is reflected. So is it with people. Each affects the other, and so on *ad infinitum*.

I am here because of my parents and they because of theirs.

In ten generations you have so and so many people involved. In thirty generations you have, I believe, 100,000,000 people involved. And we are still at the beginning of human life on this earth.

Now we have myself here as a result of all this past, and you. All this past effort is crystallized in each of us. This is the temporal aspect.

Now for the spatial. I eat rice grown by this man, wear clothes made by those men, and so on. It is estimated that 100,000 people are involved in keeping me going *now*. You may say: "*I* went to Osaka by train," but think of the people involved in producing that train and making that journey possible. (Who then went to Osaka?)

So the Zen attitude is to bow in all directions to give thanks to all. And if you understand this gratitude you try to serve society. This is the life of what we call the Bodhisattva, the man who understands.

The way of the adult is to bow in all directions. Then you are living according to the teaching. A Bodhisattva takes a vow to devote himself to society for all his lives.

So you have Manju, Fugen, and Kannon, the central Bodhisattvas (of intuitive wisdom, harmony, and kindness) in the Zen philosophy. Of these, Fugen is the chief one.

If you understand the thanks that you owe to all, you give your life to service. However, this must not be confused with pantheism because you are not worshipping a spirit in things. Mainly, however, it must not be confused with pantheism because that confusion leads Westerners to think that Buddhism is idolatry.

Epilogue

THE zen student is told to feel the force of the universe behind him. One day he does. His intense concentration in *zazen* leads to this step, for it is a concentration of his energies. From here he goes on to sense more and more deeply that the pillow on which he sits for *zazen* is helping him, that *it* is part of *his* work. Eventually he merges with the pillow. Other distinctions between subjective and objective disappear. He feels at one with the things and people around him, ultimately with the whole world. His growing strength is not dissipated by this realization of identity. It is rather freed thereby: to bring him out of the past and future of his memories and plans into the immediate present.

The zen student then increasingly has a sensation as of awakening abruptly from a daydream. The world about him is suddenly sharply in focus at these moments. During them he feels the blinding effect of the illusions from which he ordinarily suffers. He may describe this in various ways. "I am in touch with reality." "I have got beneath the idea of self." "I and reality are one." "There is no self. There is only reality. Appearance and emptiness are the same; the relative and the absolute."

At other times he may see that this experience is none other than a feeling of calm. Indeed, it is calmness itself. He finds himself simply and fully in the workaday and matter-of-fact world, the world of common sense in which he had always lived but with which, he now sees, he had been strangely out of touch.

With *zazen* the student may come to realize, too, that there are many ways of talking about that which he is now experiencing. Most of these descriptions sound mysterious, although he finds the experiences themselves quite natural. He also sees that these experiences can be put into words for those who have had them. They can be grasped by thought, but they cannot be arrived at by thought. They are ineffable only for those who have not had them. It has been otherwise misleading to speak of these experiences as ineffable.

However, these insights pale by comparison with the student's realization of his oneness with reality, the experience of being in the immediate present. At this moment he sees that theory is opaque. Naught compares with this direct awareness of things, an awareness so complete that he becomes the things he perceives. They are like lovers in union. He is in another world and yet it is the same world, illuminated now by full consciousness. He understands it. There are no mysteries.

A profound change has come about. The moral precept to "love thy neighbor as thyself" suddenly appears to him as a description of fact and no longer as a command. With the disappearance of the distinction between nature and self has gone the distinction between the "is" and the "ought." In his egolessness, fact and value merge. To be moral is natural, and it is natural to be moral. A veneration for all things suffuses the man. Gone are the doubts and the fears; in their place, a willingness to live and to let live.

Yet the experience of morality seems natural. There is nothing extraordinary about it. It is as though he had returned to something that always was but from which he had departed into a world of phantasms.

The matter is simple and still it is not easy. The awareness of reality and the insight into the naturalness of morals are steps which the zen student takes in *zazen*. Taking these steps does not mean that he will any the better practice this morality, for the insight must be ever deepened. He will someday come to feel it and then to be it and then to live the insight, but this will take years of hard work and unremitting effort. The insight at the surface is one thing. In its deep it is another. As Spinoza said, all things excellent are as difficult as they are rare.

The reader may leave the matter here. Or, rather, he may turn to the matter which is *zazen*. On the other hand, the foregoing considerations can be refocused by relating *zazen* to two philosophic issues. They appear below in the order in which they occur above. It is not necessarily the order in which they manifest themselves to the reflective individual.

One philosophic problem is the metaphysical. What is reality? Metaphysics, the answering of this question, is the science of being (ultimate reality). This is to say that it is the knowledge of being. To put it more simply, a person has become interested in the metaphysical question when he has come to ask: What is it all about? I no longer know my way around? The way to this knowledge in the West has been through reason. Today it is called science.

Reflection shows, however, that science does not tell us what reality is like. This realization is not new and has been expressed in many ways. In modern terminology it may be phrased as follows. From the Greek view of science as descriptive or representative of reality there has been a shift to the pragmatic or instrumental view. We see now that science gives us control over nature by enabling us to predict, but its theories and concepts are constructs which do not inform. They are inventions not discoveries. One has only to compare the theory that the earth moves around the sun with the theory that the sun moves around the earth to see what is involved here. Which "describes" the world as it is?

This realization has led men to despair of *knowing* reality. The despair, as implied above, is not new and it has differently affected each individual who feels it. It was in the work of the

Greek Skeptics (300 B.C.–200 A.D.) and it led them to retreat from the world. At that time it prepared the West intellectually for Christianity with its message of the divine revelation of the ultimate reality. Hume voiced the despair, but was optimistic. If we cannot know, we cannot. Meanwhile, let us live. Kant said that we cannot know the thing-in-itself. The world we know is a phenomenal world. He counseled against trying to know more than this. In the twentieth century, metaphysics is either despised or it is treated as the science of language, the study of the categories of being instead of the study of being. We are once removed from reality, immersed in a study of the subjective, rootless.

Today the despair is deeply felt. The philosophy of existentialism is an attempt to break out of it. The more common reaction is to follow Kant's advice. He saw the urge to understand as the urge that leads to science. But he thought that it can be carried too far and that, when it is uncontrolled, it results in nonsense. The contemporary form of following the advice to control the urge is to ignore it. Metaphysics is dead, we say; or, at best, it is the study of the relations of sublanguages within a language to each other.

What is the bearing of *zazen* on the metaphysical problem? Throughout the long history of the problem there has been a tenuous tradition according to which there is a way of knowing other than the rational. This is the way of the mystic. The practice of *zazen* is in this tradition. The practice is a way of knowing reality other than the scientific. It is a direct way, unmediated by concepts and theories. It leads through the self to nature. To know thyself is finally to know reality. For the practitioner of *zazen* metaphysics begins where *zazen* does. It ends in understand*ing,* not knowledge.

Some minor remarks must be made in this connection. One is that the practice of *zazen* is precisely that—a practice. There is a definite procedure for it. The zen student does *this* and *that* during *zazen.* It can be taught. In this respect *zazen* is out of most of the mystical tradition in the West. For in that tradition, at least popularly, there is little if any precise instruction. The thing has seldom been made practical.

This leads to saying further that there is presented here no glib solution to the metaphysical problem. To say that *zazen* bears on the problem carries us no further than one is borne by the advice to go to college. The long hard work remains. The metaphysical problem has ever been one of the most difficult problems. It remains so with *zazen.*

Finally, according to the Western mystical tradition the mystical experience is the union of the individual with God. In this union the Source and the person retain their identities. In the *zazen* experience the individual merges with reality and loses his identity. There is, then, this important difference between Western mysticism and *zazen:* the former is theological, the latter naturalistic. That is to say, the zen practitioner experiences a complete identification with reality. He becomes egoless. One of his steps takes him beyond the experience of the Western mystic. There is for him finally no dualism, not even that of God and the world.

Another philosophic problem is the moral one. It occurs in many forms. In the *Republic* Plato raised it by having Thrasymachus ask: How would you behave if you were immune to punishment? The question is sharpened by referring to a mythical hero, Gyges, who was given a ring by the gods that would make him invisible when he wore it. With this ring Gyges conquered the enemies of his people. Suppose that you were given such a ring, one which would enable you to do as you please without regard for consequences. How would you live your life?

Thrasymachus thinks that the answer is obvious. You would act solely in self-interest. It is, Thrasymachus believes, the natural condition of men to promote their own existences. The strong get away with this and keep the weak in line by a system of laws. There is no morality except by conventions that represent the interests of the strong. In a democracy the "strong" are the weak who band together.

This is a view with great appeal for anyone who has come to reflect on the moral issue. What the good is for men is an extraordinarily difficult question. Thrasymachus's view makes it simple, or gets rid of it, by reducing morals to psychology and making a science of the matter. The *Republic* is Plato's attempt to combat this view. It is, in other words, his attempt to show that men can be naturally moral and to show what that morality is. The attempt proceeds by a line of reasoning that concludes that men become moral when they attain to the vision of the good, in Plato's terms, when they see the Idea of the Good. The *Republic* is more than this. It is also Plato's attempt to convey the Idea of the Good to his readers.

Plato was both successful and unsuccessful as a philosopher. He himself became a good man. He had the Idea of the Good. It is doubtful, however, whether the *Republic* successfully answers Thrasymachus's question. At least, philosophers since Plato have argued whether it does. They have even disputed about the nature of what Plato called the Good—the moral.

These matters constitute moral theory which may be regarded as the attempt to answer Thrasymachus's question. When the religious answer has not been accepted, the attempt has been conducted in the manner in which Plato proceeded in the *Republic*. Plato tried to answer the question rationally. This resulted in a particular moral theory. Since his day there have been many moral theories, and sometimes the rational approach has issued in moral skepticism.

The experiences in which *zazen* results suggests that there is another way of answering Thrasymachus's question. It is a radically empirical way. Paradoxically, it is also "rational"; for the zen student "sees" the answer to the moral problem, and his reason is used in the larger process. He can, furthermore, assure anyone that if he will but perform the "experiment," he too will perceive the answer.

Plato was right. There is knowledge of the Good. The fact that there is is the answer to Thrasymachus. The question remains: How is this knowledge obtained? The practice of *zazen* indicates that the way to it may be direct and not through reason, although reason may help here and there. As with the metaphysical question so with the moral: the answer to it lies in direct knowing and not in science. Once again: this statement does not imply that the requisite knowledge has been made any easier.

It may be said by the skeptic that a man can discover the good in himself because it has been laid in there by long training received at the hands of society. Something like Thrasymachus's explanation in terms of conventional morality, therefore, still holds. This is to be concerned with explanations, however, and not with realities. As I have remarked, an interest in explanations is all very well, but explanations should not be confused with the stuff being explained.

It might be said, in conclusion, that these remarks are by way of being a report. Neither the metaphysical nor the moral question has been answered. And proof is not given that *zazen* is the way to the answers to these questions. I have tried simply to express in one fashion some of the experiences that the zen student has in the *practice of Zen*.

Notes

Chapter 1

1.   In Japanese, meditation is called 'zazen.' Throughout this book I
am not concerned to say that *zazen* is the essence of Zen Buddhism
in the sense that no other Buddhists practice it but only in the
sense that *zazen* is essential to Zen Buddhism. As a matter of fact,
a serious Buddhist of any sect may practice *zazen,* although by
no means all Buddhists do, and there are other people than Buddhists who practice some form of meditation. The Buddha himself, long before the development of Zen Buddhism, practiced
zazen and constantly counseled his disciples to work assiduously
at it. Thus, that which characterizes Zen Buddhism is the *systematic
and rigorous* use of *zazen* by its adherents.

There are a number of secondary characteristics of Zen Buddhism
that are also important in distinguishing it from other forms of
Buddhism. For example, early in the development of Zen in China
its teachers virtually gave up the use of sutras and lengthy dis-
courses in their instructions, resorting instead to such other devices
as pithy stories or remarks and the use of blows and other forms
of physical treatment. This has marked Zen teaching ever since,
even though a partial return to the use of long documents later
occurred. Further, Zen architecture and customs are characterized
by an extreme severity and simplicity that serves to mark them
off from those of other forms of Buddhism. There is, too, a sort
of hard-headed practicality about the Zen Buddhist that is characteristic. In the case of some Buddhists of other sects who do

practice *zazen,* only the absence of these secondary attributes would serve to distinguish them from the Zen Buddhist.

D. T. Suzuki wrote somewhere that three paths to enlightenment are offered in Buddhism: insight (*prajna*), morality, and meditation (*dhyana* or *zen*). He also wrote (in *Living by Zen* [Tokyo: Sanseido Press, 1949], p. 193) that *prajna* not *dhyana* is the essence of Zen Buddhism despite what scholars have said about the etymology of the word 'zen.' Professor Suzuki had reasons for this, which will be discussed later. The result is that he has emphasized insight. However, if practice without insight is blind, insight without practice is baseless. It is the practice of Zen of which the West must now become aware if the growing interest in Zen Buddhism is to be anything more than dilettante.

2.   The word 'roshi' is literally equivalent to 'venerable teacher.' It has been translated by 'master' or 'Zen Master.' I use the term 'roshi' because 'master' is misleading. A *roshi* is a master of the practice of Zen Buddhism and a master at teaching it, but he is more. He is a man with great force of will and intellect who has not only completed Zen studies with a *roshi* but has received from his teacher the seal of approval that allows him in turn to teach. Not all those who complete their studies and are accomplished practitioners of Zen Buddhism have the other attributes that mark a man or woman as a *roshi*. A *roshi* is, however, also less than a "master." He is a practical, common-sensed, hard worker who brooks no nonsense and forms no band of sycophantic followers. To render 'roshi' by 'master' causes this hard-headed practicality to be lost sight of. Many Japanese words like 'roshi' are usually printed in English texts with a bar over the 'o.' I am omitting these bars for simplicity. The purpose of this book is philosophical, not scholarly.

3.   Dogen was the founder of the Japanese Soto Zen Sect, which is by far the largest of the three Zen Buddhist sects in Japan. The others are the Rinzai and the Obaku Sects. The Soto Sect is characterized by the emphasis of its adherents on *zazen* as being, together with the observance of the Buddhist moral code, the sole method of achieving enlightenment. The only other Zen Buddhist sect of which we hear much in the West is the Rinzai Sect. In-

148

deed, it is, due to the efforts of Suzuki, the only Zen sect of which
we hear much. This sect practices the koan exercise as an aid to
zazen. It is the sect to which reference is made throughout the
sequel.

There were five streams of Zen teaching in China originally, but
all, with the exception of the Chinese Soto, were absorbed into
Chinese Rinzai Zen by the Ming dynasty (A.D. 1368–1644); and
during that period Chinese Soto Zen was also absorbed into the
Rinzai Sect. Present-day Chinese Ch'an, though often referred to
as Rinzai Zen, is really an amalgamation of not only all the
previous types of Zen but of other Buddhist sects as well. Japanese
Soto is decidedly different from the earlier Chinese Soto Zen.
Dogen was an original thinker, and, though he received his seal
of approval from a Soto master in China, he changed the methods
and practices as well as many of the views of Soto to conform to
his own ideas. Japenese Soto Zen is now beginning to make efforts
to interest Westerners.

4.   Daisetz Teitaro Suzuki, *Essays in Zen Buddhism (Third Series)*,
(London: Rider and Company, 1953), p. 306.

Chapter 2

1.   I should like to remark that I, who have gone only shallowly into
the onion, can speak of these things precisely because the matter
is like an onion. The understanding of the directions is easy. It
is only the following of them which is hard.

The first anecdote is from Suzuki, *Essays in Zen Buddhism (Second
Series)*, (Boston: The Beacon Press, 1952), p. 17.

The second anecdote is from *Zen Flesh and Zen Bones, A
Collection of Zen and pre-Zen Writings,* trans. and compiled
by Paul Reps and Nyogen Sensaki (Tokyo: Chas. E. Tuttle Co.,
1958), p. 67.

Chapter 3

1.   The code, incidentally, is strikingly similar to that embodied in
the Ten Commandments. The only important difference is that

there is in it no reference to God. The basis of the code is: Love thy neighbor as thyself.

2. There is an aspect of formal *zazen* that cannot or should not be extended to certain other activities. It is the concentration on breathing, which is one means by which the zen student learns to control his mind. Successful use of the breathing exercise can lead to such deep concentration that the student becomes completely unaware of his surroundings. Zen students sometimes speak of this as "having the mind drop down" into the guts, the center of their beings. Clearly this would be an undesirable thing to have happen while driving an automobile.

    I have distinguished formal and informal *zazen*. Although the word 'zen' is often said to be an abbreviation of '*zazen*,' strictly speaking '*zazen*' means 'sitting (za) meditation (zen)' to differentiate it from meditation walking, gardening, etc., or what I have called informal *zazen*.

3. The zen student is the meditating student, the one practicing *zazen*. There is, as noted in the Preface, a curious mystique forming about the word 'Zen,' one which enfolds its user in something unimaginable. It helps to get back to the facts to use 'Zen' as an adjective without capitalizing it.

Chapter 4

1. The rules are excerpted from a series translated by Professor Reiho Masunaga, which appears in his book *The Soto Approach to Zen* (Tokyo: Layman Buddhist Society Press, 1958), Chapter 8.

    Keizan does not sound typical. He seems to have been awfully worried about temptation.

Chapter 6

1. *Essays in Zen Buddhism (First Series)*, (New York: Harper and Bros., 1949), p. 23.

2. *Living by Zen*, pp. 56–57.

    Presumably Ryutan was practicing *zazen* all this time. The Zen Buddhist takes *zazen* so much for granted that he means by "instructions" lectures or some other aid to *zazen*. Tenno had been giving him a form of the silent treatment, further examples of which follow in this chapter.

3.   *Living by Zen,* p. 56.
4.   *Ibid.,* pp. 92–93. 'Daruma' is Japanese for 'Bodhidharma,' the name of the founder of Zen Buddhism in China. Often both names are used as symbols for the Buddha.
5.   *Essays in Zen Buddhism (First Series),* p. 262.

Chapter 7

1.   Koans are not employed by all Zen Buddhists. Their use appeared relatively late in the history of Zen Buddhism. And there are now, and have been since the inception of these devices, stern critics of their value. Some of these have maintained that *sanzen* and the koan are worse than useless, that they are hindrances to the practice of Zen Buddhism. Of course, it may be that what works for some does not work for others. However, these differences of opinion are not part of my concern here, which is to look at *zazen* from another angle.

Furthermore, there are other ways of looking at the koan exercise than that developed in this chapter. Suzuki, for example, regards it as a way of bringing meditation to a point of intense concentration that makes possible a step forward. He is also of the opinion that the exercise was introduced to combat two deadly enemies of Zen Buddhism: the notion that its practice is mere quietism and the notion that it can be grasped intellectually. Again, however, these differences of interpretation do not affect the function of this chapter which is that of calling attention to *zazen* in yet another way. For those interested, please see the chapter on the Koan Exercise in *Essays in Zen Buddhism (Second Series),* especially pp. 82–84. (Reading is all right so long as it does not interfere with *zazen,* though it usually does.)

The koan exercise, incidentally, shows the activity that is also characteristic of the practice of Zen. *Zazen* is not *mere* sitting, as will become apparent when we get more deeply into it. The student is always working at it, using koans to cut through his ego.

This activity characterizes *zazen* and it characterizes the successful zen student, who is an active and alert person and by no means passive and retiring.

2. A common mistake here is, when stuck, to go to a book for help. This will not work because the answer to the student's question is in him. . . . So with the question: What is Zen? Don't read. Sit.

3. It is misleading to speak of *solving* a koan, for it is not a problem in the sense that a problem in algebra is a problem, although at first the Westerner inevitably tends to treat a koan this way. What *is* the sound of one hand? And you think of various tricks. 'Passing a koan' is better, and 'analysis with a koan' is better than 'analysis of a koan,' for work with a koan is both physical and mental work. Like *zazen* it is an affair of the whole person and not simply of his head.

    On the other hand, delightfully enough, all koans have classic answers. There is not one answer for you and one for me and one for the other fellow; no such thing as *my* answer. The student has not penetrated the matter deeply enough when he thinks this, which is a bit of information for which I am indebted to a person who has had years of zen study.

4. Interestingly enough, the student may be brought back to the *mu* koan at various times in his study, and he may finish with this koan. This also shows the step-like character of zen study and the fact that getting an "answer" to a koan is no mere intellectual affair but one that involves the student's body, his emotions and all, as well as his mind. Without the *practice* the matter is empty.

5. This too shows how physical the study of Zen is. And don't university students leave a lecture with notebooks clutched in hands?

Chapter 8

1. *Zen Flesh and Zen Bones*, pp. 90–91.

    It may be noted of the connection between Zen and the *samurai* that they adopted some of its physical discipline but had no interest in its spiritual component. A similar observation may be made for the so-called influence of Zen on other Japanese institutions. In fact, as Mrs. Sasaki and Mr. Blyth have pointed out, the influence is usually in the reverse direction.

It might also be said that zen study *can* result in remarkable experiences, even though they are incidental to it. One of the more annoying of such experiences is self-hypnosis in the course of which the student convinces himself that he has made a step forward when in fact he has not. If he should stop his studies at that time, he would give a curious report of Zen Buddhism.

Chapter 9

1. The story is from Mrs. Sasaki. I have paraphrased her personal recitation of it, which subsequently appeared in *Rinzai Zen Study for Foreigners in Japan* (Kyoto: The First Zen Institute of America in Japan, 1960). Mrs. Sasaki has also published *Zen: A Religion* (1958) and *Zen: A Method for Religious Awakening* (1959). All these essays are available at The First Zen Institute of America, 156 Waverly Place, New York, N.Y.

2. This example can be altered to one which illuminates koans. They are the knives with which the edges are cut, and the student is the apprentice, the *roshi* the master carpenter.

3. That remark about rushing ahead to get the answers to the koans and forgetting the practice is worth thinking about. *Zazen* is a matter of spiritual development and takes time. In a way this applies word for word to living. One thinks that he can know all the answers quickly and that then all will be well. He does not even see at first that being told the answers does not mean that he understands them; that is, can use them. The father says to the adolescent, "You will understand this when you grow up." "Nonsense," the boy thinks, "I know what you are saying." But he does not. He knows the meanings of the words but does not understand.

One gets here a perspective on Zen Buddhism. Working with a koan may be likened to living. In living one constantly encounters paradoxes. There is the problem of evil, for example, and more concretely the matter of having children. It is clear that they are at the same time a blessing and a nuisance. You cannot do without them and you cannot live with them. Eventually, however, most of us learn to. Some people do so easily, almost naturally, others with difficulty, some never. So in a koan there is a paradox. Sheer ingenuity will not solve it. (It has been misleading to say that Zen Buddhism is the intellectual form of Buddhism, although it is not false.) No matter how ingenious you are with children you have to learn to live with them. Or take some dodge and do not. Not that there is not a great deal to be said for dodges. They are a kind of "solution," though as such they resemble drugs as solutions to problems. The training, the practice that goes with a koan is like the experience that life inflicts upon us. We can grin and bear it and sweat it through, or we can quit. And just as the paradox in a koan disappears when the koan is seen through, so do the paradoxes of life. It is not that children are difficult. It is that we have a time learning to live with them.

4. If you do not have a pliable body, you do not have a pliable mind? What of the vigorous intellectual, seventy and still the leader in his field, who could not bend down and touch his toes to save his life? Answer: His mind is not pliable in the way which is meant here. A mind may be logical and quick, but not open to new ideas, and to change. It cannot "solve" a koan, that is, see things about itself.

Chapter 10

1. The building in a temple grounds, set aside for the purpose, in which Zen students practice *zazen*.

2. *Essays in Zen Buddhism (Second Series)*, p. 148.

3. The first story is from *Zen Flesh and Zen Bones,* p. 19. The second is from *Essays in Zen Buddhism (First Series)*, p. 210. There it is also related that Hui-neng, upon the advice of his teacher, spent several years in seclusion in the mountains after he obtained enlightenment. Only then did he come out into the world.

Chapter 11

1. Furthermore, the facts that counting during *zazen* gives the mind something to hang onto and that the koans perform a similar function (another of their uses) show that the zen student is not supposed to fall into mere quiescence with his practice.

2. I am indebted to Mrs. Sasaki for the information about the Zen cave.

3. The point of stressing insight or the mental aspect of the matter is made clearer by a monk's remark that a pyramid without an apex is no pyramid. Contrariwise, neither is it one without a base.

4. This is not a custom in many other sects.

The references to Zen as your "everyday life," however, have themselves been misleading. In reading them one easily thinks that it is *his* everyday life of which mention is made. It is not. It is the everyday life of the enlightened man, that is, of the man who is successfully practicing *zazen*. Otherwise, of course, it is the everyday life of everyone. Those who have not awakened to it do not know that it cannot be *their* everyday life, that is, that a profound change must take place within the individual before it can be *his* everyday life.

On the other hand, the "everyday life" saying is important, for it helps to show that there is nothing mysterious about the matter.

A similar misunderstanding can arise in connection with the stories of a master who thunders, "The Buddha is the one who stands before me." Since he seems to be talking to a disciple, the unwary reader is likely to think that the master is referring to a beginner with that 'the one who stands.' He is not. He is referring to another master or to one well along the line. Otherwise, of course, it is true that the disciple is a Buddha *if he would only realize it*. But that realization takes years of practice. In less exotic terms this is to say that every man is an enlightened man if he would only realize it. But that realization cannot be brought about by thought or by simply willing it. It takes years of practice, years of physical as well as mental effort. . . . I am in-

debted to Walter Novick for the point about who the person is
when a master is said to speak of him as the Buddha.

5.   *Essays in Zen Buddhism (First Series)*, p. 374.
It should be remarked that 'Buddha' is not a proper name, although it is always capitalized in English. It is used in phrases
like 'the Buddha' and 'a Buddha' and means the enlightened one
or an enlightened man. 'The Buddha' usually refers to the man
Siddhartha Gautama of the Sakya clan in India, the first of the
teachers of enlightenment. History has it that he abandoned all
methods and teachings except *zazen* to attain his enlightenment. He was also, before he undertook his spiritual adven-
ture, a leader of his clan. Hence, he is sometimes referred to as
Sakyamuni.

Chapter 12

1.   Rinzai (died 867), disciple of Huang Po, was the founder of the
sect that bears his name. The following excerpts are paraphrased
from *Ch'an and Zen Teaching (Series Two)*, (London: Rider and
Co., 1961), pp. 84–110. Luk employs Rinzai's Chinese names, 'I
Hsuan' and 'Lin Chi.' For the sake of uniformity with the present
text I am using his Japanese name, 'Rinzai.'
In *Ch'an and Zen Teaching* Luk's commentaries on the *Record*
appear as footnotes. Here they are placed in the text and labeled
'Commentaries.' Commentaries on ancient texts are a common
form of Zen teaching.
As I have indicated, old Zen texts are in a peculiar common-folk
dialect. As a purely scholarly translation, Luk's does not reflect
this vernacular and the frequent coarseness of the speech. It thus
misses some of the vigor of the *Rinzai Record*. Therefore, I have
paraphrased the interchanges that follow to give them more of the
active strength that characterizes the originals.

2.   Zen must be transmitted from person to person. The relation of
the master to the pupil is like that of the father to the child. The
monk here failed to keep up with Rinzai.
Rinzai's 'Ho!' ('kwats' in Japanese) is variously used: like a

sword to cut away error, to test, sometimes to show enlightenment.

3. This is an exchange in which each participant shows his enlightenment. The old teachers were fond of these "duels" in which they tested each other.

Koans can test enlightenment as well as help it. A *roshi* can use a koan during *sanzen* to test the student. If the latter has made a step, he will not falter with the new blow.

Notice how Joshu counters Rinzai's initial question by calling attention to the washing of his feet, a simple everyday act. Rinzai's question has become a koan.

4. Neither Rinzai nor San Sheng struck the monk to make him mad. A Zen temple is not a lunatic asylum. The blows were marks of kindness, a Zen trait.

5. There was little need for words in that interchange. Each master was *showing* the audience reality instead of trying to tell them what it is. The *performance* was the sermon.

6. Why do you worry about who won this interchange? Didn't Ma Ku show that he understood?

7. The second monk showed guts, and therefore something of Zen, in repeating the question and thus entering the lists.

The case of the first monk is open to a different interpretation. When he asked Rinzai about the essence of Buddhism, Rinzai raised his stick. He answered with an action. The Buddha once simply raised a flower to propound his teaching. The disciple who understood merely smiled. And so the first monk said: "Ho!" instead of: "That's clear. I understand." Why then did Rinzai hit him? As a mark of approval!

As with the 'Ho's' so with the blows; they have a variety of uses. A Zen story will explain this as well as Luk's reference in his commentary to the "illusory" stick. A Zen *roshi* once handed a fan to one of his students, asking: "What is this?" The student handed it back, saying: "A fan." The *roshi* frowned and handed the fan to another student with the same question. This man took the fan and, without a word, scratched his back with it, stirred the *hibachi* with it, opened it, fanned himself; then, placing a gift on it, he handed it back to the *roshi*. The *roshi* smiled.

The first student's answer was simple and straightforward. It showed, however, that he was stuck with the concept of a fan. He still saw the fan through the medium of his idea of it. It was thus an "illusory" object for him.

The story of the fan is so instructive that I repeat it later.

8.   Gold powder is, nevertheless, gold powder. Sutras and meditation are invaluable, provided that a person does not cling to them, become too attached to them. Rinzai, therefore, had double reason for acknowledging Wang's degree of enlightenment.

Chapter 13

1.   These "sayings" are not in Rinzai's words. They are liberal paraphrases from Mr. Luk's translation of the second part of the *Rinzai Record* in *Ch'an and Zen Teaching (Second Series)*, pp. 110–26.

If it be asked why Rinzai did not simply give the advice to sit quietly, an answer is: it had already been given. These sayings, as has been noted for all utterances by a Zen teacher, are aids for carrying out the basic advice.

Readers of the works of the later Wittgenstein will notice the striking resemblance between some of Rinzai's sayings and remarks by Wittgenstein. I have in mind Rinzai's "Nothing has a nature of its own—though names delude us in this" and "There is no fixed teaching. All I can provide is an appropriate medicine for a particular ailment." Cf. Wittgenstein's, 'The tendency to look for something in common to all the entities which we commonly subsume under a general term.' (*The Blue and Brown Books*, p. 17.) Also: 'There is not *a* philosophical method, though there are indeed methods, like different therapies.' (*Philosophical Investigations*, Section 133.)

Chapter 14

1.   The lay disciple or student may have an occupation outside the temple. He may, for example, be working for a degree at a university. In such cases he does not, except for the first year, live in

the temple. Instead he comes morning and evening for *zazen,* and *sanzen* with the *roshi.*

2. A *zendo* is a long rectangular building, a hall, with raised portions six feet wide and three feet high running along both long walls. These are called *tan.* The student meditates on them and sleeps on them at night. That is why the *tan* are six feet wide. In the *zendo* the student has a spot three feet by six to himself. It is his world. At one end of the hall is a shrine with a statue of some Bodhisattva in it, in most cases of Manjusri, the Bodhisattva of Intuitive Wisdom. Occasionally Kasyapa is enshrined.

3. Begging is another aid to *zazen.* In addition to its economic value for support of the temple, it teaches the beggar humility and the donor self-denial.

Chapter 15

1.

THE YEMMEI KWANNON TEN-CLAUSE SUTRA

(Adoration to) Kwannon!
Adoration to the Buddha!
To the Buddha we are related
In terms of cause and effect.
Depending on the Buddha, the Dharma and the Sangha,
(Nirvana is possible which is) eternal, ever-blessed,
Autonomous and free from defilements.
Every morning our thoughts are on Kwanzeon,
Every evening our thoughts are on Kwanzeon.
Every thought issues from the mind,
Every thought is not separated from the mind.

Suzuki, *Manual of Zen Buddhism* (London: Rider, 1957), p. 16.
People react similarly to the idea of psychoanalysis. There is a fear or suspicion of it. Samuel Goldwyn is reported to have remarked that anyone who goes to an analyst ought to have his head examined.

2. Other forms of it occur to one who is already accustomed to Oriental trappings, which seem to a Westerner to be that to which he is reacting.

Chapter 16

1.   Sources for that which follows are: *The Cat's Yawn* (New York: The First Zen Institute of America, Inc., 1947); various Buddhist society quarterlies; conversations with Mrs. Sasaki and members of the Institute in Kyoto, particularly Gary Snyder; talks with Ruth McCandless; and talks with Goto Roshi.

2.   The author of *Zen in the Art of Archery* and, posthumously published, *The Method of Zen.*

Chapter 17

1.   The West's philosophic theories must sound as strange to the Oriental as the sutras do to Western ears. In fact they sound as queer as the sutras to most Westerners. For too often have they been mistaken for science, their own practical value thereby being missed.

Chapter 18

1.   Only *roshis* can conduct *sanzen,* which is essential for full development in *zazen.* This is not simply a matter of authority. A person with less training than that which is required to be a *roshi* can lead a student hopelessly astray, for the path he is following is complicated and crisscrossed. Until its end is reached, one who has not reached it can go in circles. How did the first travelers arrive safely? They were geniuses.

2.   The term 'ego' is used in a special and technical sense by psychoanalysts. It is used with a broader meaning by Buddhists and still more broadly by the layman. In this paragraph it has been used first in the psychoanalytic sense, then in the Buddhist, and finally in such a way as to include both uses.

Chapter 19

1.   *Zen Flesh and Zen Bones,* pp. 83, 84.

2.   As has been noted, this void is not mere void.

In the fact that the void is not a mere void the difference between the positivist and the Zen Buddhist comes out. That is, the questions are not merely meaningless. The difference also appears in the fact that the Zen Buddhist has seen that the questions do have answers.

Readers of philosophy may note that there is something odd about Descartes' proof for the existence of the external world in *Meditation VI*. Logically the proof fails. As a resolver of doubt, it succeeded—for Descartes. He had come to question whether the external world exists. After this "proof" he was able to say, "Of course it does."

In another tradition than the skeptical, Western philosophers have sought answers to the fundamental questions by rational means. This has apparently resulted in various and contradictory philosophical systems. However, when you get below the surfaces of these, down in through them, they turn out to be routes to something strikingly like that at which the Zen Buddhist arrives. Descartes started with "hyperbolic doubt" and came to believe that he and the world existed. Spinoza struggled through the metaphysical portion of his *Ethics* to a final section called "Of Human Freedom," in which he concluded, among other things: "In proportion as the mind understands more things . . . [it] stands in less fear of death" (Prop. XXXVIII); and "All things excellent are as difficult as they are rare."

It appears that both the empirical and the rational traditions have been right, though only the original thinkers in each tradition achieved practical as well as theoretical results, becoming philosophers thereby.

3.   This is not so pretentious as it sounds at first blush. (a) The answers have always been there. (b) It is one thing to set them down and another to understand them. Remember the onion. (c) Even if a person has some of the answers, the doubt which gives rise to these questions may not be stilled. It can appear in other questions. (d) Finally, one has only to read to get the verbal answers.

4.   This illustration is reported in many places. The quotation is from William Barrett's introduction to his selection from Suzuki's writings in the Anchor Books of Doubleday.

The illustration has not been reported fully. In the original, it forms the basis of a koan. Of it the question is asked: What is the difference between the three stages?

Chapter 21

1. *Living by Zen,* pp. 92–93. It is easy to get the impression from these stories that the matter is simple and that anyone can do it. Gensha's instruction appears clear, easily understood. However, Gensha's pupils who are hard at work at *zazen* find it difficult.

Chapter 22

1. This and the following chapter are from notes based on lectures given me by Goto Roshi the week before I left Japan. They were his way of capping my introduction to zen study.
2. In response to a question, he said that it is the *ideas* of these things of which one is trying to be rid.
3. He has pointed out at another time that contradictions are built into us by living, giving as an example: a child wants something and his father says that he cannot have it.